The Elephant in the Bedroom

Automobile Dependence & Denial

The Elephant in the Bedroom

Pg 1

Impacts on the
Economy and Environment

Stanley I. Hart & Alvin L. Spivak

New Paradigm Books
Pasadena, California

New Paradigm Books
P. O. Box 60008
Pasadena, California 91116 - U.S.A.
Tel: (818) 792-6123; FAX (818) 792-2121

Cover design — Juan Carlos Fernandez

Printed in the U.S.A. on acid-free paper.

Library of Congress Cataloging-in-Publication Data

Hart, Stanely I., 1918-
    Automobile dependence & denial : the elephant in the bedroom
: impacts on the economy and environment / by Stanley I. Hart &
Alvin L. Spivak.
      p.   cm.
    ISBN 0-932727-65-4 (lib. bdg.) -- ISBN 0-932727-64-6 (pbk.)
    1. Transportation, Automotive--United States. 2. Traffic safety--
United States. I. Title.
HE5623.H38 1993
363.12'5'0973--DC20   92-41269
                                                  CIP

To: Mary Ann

CONTENTS

Summary. The condition of society and the economy as affected by our automobile-dependence created by heavy subsidies: parking, operating space, government costs.

Transit firms robbed of patronage—subsidies needed for survival—middle-class commuters excluded from public transit use—only young, old, poor and the handicapped ride buses.

Parking and operating space; real estate and improvements costs impact the economy.

Local governments, business, manufacturing
and retail trade; police and fire protection, traffic engineering, roads, hospitals, courts, etc.

Snobbery and machismo—luxury and macho
cars and trucks, (diversion of funds from more
productive uses), macho driving (tailgating,
slaloming, etc.). The gratuitous destruction of
the American family. Sometimes a cigar is only
a cigar—sometimes a car is only transportation.

One death every ten minutes; a serious injury
every ten seconds—40 to 50,000 deaths; 400 to
500,000 serious injuries and maimings.

Engineers must play a game in which "build"
means that their careers may be fulfilled. Developers, highway engineers and political leaders find common ground.

Contents

A rational basis for judging the benefits and
the effectiveness of our transportation system.

Solutions to the transportation/air pollution
problem are proposed which do not solve the
problem of the automobile—self-defeating.

Raise the price of automobile/truck ownership
and operation to the equivalence of its cost to
society—either by an increased fuel tax and a license fee or an electronic toll collection (parking, highway-use tax) device—the yield used to
reduce, perhaps eliminate, property, sales and/
or social security taxes.

The relationship of the environment to economic questions and other considerations.

INTRODUCTION

The Case for Full-Cost Pricing

The nation labors under policies which created, between the 30s and the 50s, its automobile-dependency. Until these policies are rectified, the nation's efforts to escape dependency will be frustrated by the subsidies—the free use by motorists and the trucking industry of costly urban space and municipal services. The cost of these are greater than is generally understood.

This abuse of market forces compels Americans to depend on 180 million automotive vehicles for passenger and freight transport. Although our rail systems are being rebuilt, replacing those which have been bankrupted and abandoned, the process is moving slowly.

The problem's enormity is illustrated by the following:

- Americans own and operate over 180 million automotive vehicles, 36% of all the vehicles on earth.
- The car and truck populations of the planet exceed half a billion, one-tenth the human population; its rate of increase is twice that of the human population.

- American vehicles, consume four billion barrels of oil annually, over 60% of all American oil consumption, half the world's motor fuel and 20% of the world's oil production.
- This enormous American oil consumption underpins the OPEC oil market cartel. It creates two-thirds of our trade imbalance.
- American cars and trucks produce 1 billion tons of carbon dioxide annually, plus vast amounts of nitrous oxides, CFCs, and other global warming gases.
- American cars and trucks are critical actors in the ongoing nationwide struggle with urban sprawl, traffic congestion and smog.
- Our reliance on these vehicles costs the American people, annually, 45,000 lives plus over 500,000 maiming injuries.

These are only the environmental impacts. We believe that our dependence on automotive vehicles (and the related destruction of our public transportation systems) is an essential element in our social problems—crime, ghettoization, poverty.

In addition, inadequate American household savings rates have created current difficulties in the American economy; these, too, are the result of our transportation policies. These policies (or, rather, lack of policy) have also placed our nation and our allies at risk, recently, at the hands of the Iraqi dictator, Saddam Hussein.

The world's oil market is heavily weighted by American demand for gasoline. American cars and trucks consume 20% of the world's oil as gasoline and diesel fuel. The world price of oil is, thus, directly dependent on the level of American consumption of these fuels. European and Asian per capita consumption is only one-quarter that of Americans because of more rational pricing policies.

Our adoption of similar policies could reduce consumption by three billion barrels annually, 15% of the world's total oil consumption; the effect on oil prices would be dramatic. We estimate that world oil prices would drop by at least a quarter—a direct savings to world economies of over $180 billion. It follows, therefore, that consumers of oil products, worldwide, are paying unfairly for the prodigal consumption of gasoline and diesel fuel in the United States.

How long before this American absurdity becomes a political football for European and Asian demogogues? How long will the tolerance of other nations endure?

Americans should adopt the following program:

- An immediate and substantial *decrease* in social security, property and sales taxes. This should be funded by a concurrent *increase* in the tax on motor fuel. Additional yearly decreases and increases should be made until the aggregate tax transfer has balanced these subsidies.
- It is essential that the major portion of the yield from the increased fuel tax be returned to the

public. However, a significant portion, as is useful, should be committed to the reconstruction of the nation's transit and rail systems. Some of these funds might also be used to reduce the federal budget deficit.

Unless world demand for oil can be substantially reduced, it will be impossible to achieve sustainable patterns of energy consumption and maintenance of the planet's reserve of oil. As the reservoir of oil is inexorably drawn down, the price of oil (plus pressures for costly exploratory drilling) will rise to intolerable levels. Because of American policies, the world is now dependent on the Middle East for vital supplies of energy, with all the hazard that implies. Politics in the Persian Gulf have now entered a less critical stage.

Now is the time to act.

1

AUTOMOBILE DEPENDENCY

"Most ignorance is vincible ignorance. We don't know because we don't want to know."

—Aldous Huxley

American automobile dependence is the elephant in the bedroom: the stench is overpowering, the bulk is awesome and the floor is sagging. It is destroying our world, but we do not see it because we choose not to see it; the motorist as freeloader is not an image that is acceptable given the ethos of the day.

The phrase, "The Elephant in the Bedroom," was invented by Alcoholics Anonymous to illuminate the dark area of human denial. The planners of the nation who deal with transportation, its political leaders and all other Americans as well, need to reflect on that denial. While we did not intend these conditions, we have allowed them to happen; we can correct the causes and, with apologies to A.A., we can cure the disease.

Americans, like everyone else, believe in the automobile. We see it as a prop for the economy and for the insecure ego; it represents freedom, power. We prefer not to see the waste, the dependence, the environmental and the societal abuse.

We learn in first year economics what happens when products or services become "free" goods. The market functions chaotically; demand goes through the roof. In most American cities, parking spaces, roads and freeways are free goods. Local government services to the motorist and to the trucking industry—traffic engineering, traffic control, traffic lights, police and fire protection, street repair and maintenance—are all free goods.

Most of the out-of-pocket expenses of motoring are either "sunk" or "deferred" costs because they do not, or do not seem to increase with the increased use of the vehicle. The costs of depreciation, insurance, maintenance and repairs do not act as market constraints; they tend to *increase* the tendency to drive.

Only the costs of fuel and of parking act as market constraints. Parking is frequently free and we "see" the cost of fuel as roughly equal to or less than the cost of bus fare. Thus, most of us drive to where we're going. Market constraints are effectively absent. Because the price appears to be almost zero, the demand for trips becomes almost infinite. The condition is worsened because of compulsions arising from the huge fixed costs of automobile ownership. Traffic congestion inevitably rises to the intolerable. And finally, traffic congestion becomes the only significant constraint on driving.

Under these conditions, whatever is done to increase highway capacity will be counterproductive. If we construct more highways and freeways, widen existing ones, make them more efficient using "Congestion Pricing" (charging tolls for the use of congested roads), "Smart Streets" (equipping highways and vehicles with electronic informational devices), HOV lanes (high-occupancy lanes to encourage carpooling), ramp metering or inducements to use transit or to carpool, we will only succeed in increasing congestion and air pollution.

Environmental abuse is only half the problem; by underpricing the use of automobiles, we have bankrupted the most important alternative, our public transit systems. In most American cities, we have the worst of all worlds. We have two unsatisfactory transportation systems: a failed and abusive automobile/freeway system on the one hand, and an inadequate and bankrupt bus transit system on the other. The freeway system has failed because of too much demand; the transit system because of too little. Both systems, competing for the same patrons, are heavily subsidized from the same taxpayer's pocket.

Funding for automobile/truck/highway subsidies is supplied by the community as a whole through increased property and sales taxes, swollen retail prices, decreased paychecks and profits and by increased rent. In Los Angeles, the prototypical American urban area, annual subsidies to the automobile/freeway system are measured in the tens of billions; the countervailing subsidies to keep public transit going are measured in the hundreds of millions. In effect, our own money is used to bribe us to drive our automobiles and trucks; a much smaller subsidy necessary to counteract the first, also extracted from our pockets, keeps the bus lines from going belly-up. Both subsidies are a dead weight on the economy.

This absurd distortion of our transportation market has a number of consequences; air pollution and traffic congestion are only the local manifestations. Our national economic distress (our failure to generate capital through personal savings; our trade imbalance; our federal deficit), our enormous contribution to the greenhouse effect, acid rain, ozone depletion, the toll of traffic deaths and injuries, the growing alienation of our society—all these are worse because of policies which encourage automobile use. These policies can be identified; they can also be corrected.

The Law of Supply and Demand is fully as legitimate as the laws of physics; we cannot ask or command that commuters use the bus or carpool any more than we can ask or command that their cars should take wing and fly across the city. If we wish to mitigate the congestion/air pollution and other problems associated with automobile use, we must make transit and automobiles truly and honestly competitive; the automobile/transit playing field must be leveled. That can be done only by increasing transit ridership; patronage must be increased. It is a chicken-and-egg situation. Transit is already subsidized (albeit far less than its competition); more money for subsidies will, eventually, be blocked by public indignation. Thus, transit can only be improved by removing the huge incentives which induce single-occupant driving.

A combination of user-fees could be used to recover the costs incurred by the motorist. The fuel tax could be increased; tolls could be imposed on all highways and freeways; mandatory parking fees could be levied. It is essential that all drivers comprehend the actual cost of the use of their cars or trucks by linking appropriate fees to the actual use of their vehicles; they could then make more rational choices.

These user-fees should, ideally, be revenue-neutral; the property tax and the sales tax should be markedly reduced by using the yields from user fees. One of these two regressive taxes might, usefully, be eliminated. That would correct an additional wrong; property and sales taxpayers would be relieved of an unfair tax burden.

The California Constitution, like the constitutions of most states, requires that yields from state gasoline taxes be sequestered. Federal gasoline tax yields as well as the income from excise taxes on parts and tires. are also sequestered by the federal government. This was done at the behest of automobile/highway interests determined that these funds be protected so that they are used only for highway purposes.

These funds, however, are insufficient to meet the needs of motorists and of the trucking industry. Since there is no mechanism protecting other funds, they are routinely raided at local, state and federal government levels to supplement the funds destined for highway use.

Thus, property and sales tax revenues are used to patch streets, install traffic signals and other traffic control devices, build highways and storm drains, provide police and fire protection for motorists and truck drivers, etc.

It is critical to the market process that user-fees be the *only* funds used for these purposes; prices for vehicle use should reflect actual costs. Property and sales tax yields should also be protected from raids for motorist-oriented services. Non-automobile-related police and fire protection, school districts and libraries, in particular, suffer grievously from this diversion.

There is also the question of equity. All of us—rich and poor, drivers and non-drivers alike—pay for highways, parking facilities and local automobile-related government services—but only drivers profit from their use. The poor and other non-drivers are the biggest losers; they lose even more because driving subsidies have forced the bankruptcy of the public transportation systems on which the poor and non-motorists depend.

The nation is financially strapped by the huge expense of our automobile/highway dependency. American personal savings are much lower than those of other industrial nations, handicapping our industry, depriving it of much-needed capital. Rectifying the price of motoring is one environmental project that will clearly *save* money. It would be a plus-sum game: the highways would be freed of congestion, the air would be cleaner, the economic system would be freed of a serious handicap; everyone, including motorists and truckers, would benefit.

"The cheapness of bread bears no relation to the sweat and toil that goes into making it," Gorbachev said (in a TV broadcast to the Soviet nation on May 27, 1990, imploring Soviet citizens to calm themselves in the face of the proposed shift to a market economy). *"We see how children in schoolyards play soccer using rolls (for the football)."* On another occasion, he indicated that Soviet farmers feed bread to their cattle because its subsidized price made it cheaper than the cost of silage or grain.

Our policies pertaining to the American car/truck/highway sector bear a family resemblance to those specifically designed for the economic structure of the Soviet Union. In his attempt to achieve the objectives of Marxism-Leninism, Stalin erased the market-mechanism in a blind, catastrophic leap of faith. He established the Soviet agency, Gosplan, located it in Moscow, and directed it to set, arbitrarily, the prices for each of the millions of articles sold in the vast nation. Gosplan was also required to manage factories, set standards, supply raw materials, labor and capital, and set production quotas for tens of thousands of Soviet factories, mines and collectivized farms throughout the vast Soviet empire.

History has shown that Stalin's substitution of central planning for market forces gave rise to the economics of the insane asylum. The enormously damaging consequences—wasteful use of resources, shortages of consumer and other goods and services, environmental abuse, low motivational levels in all worker and manager echelons—have now become known to the world. Its disastrous consequences led, of course, to the Gorbachev revolution and the breakup of the Soviet Union.

The efficacy of the free market for a national economy is confirmed by the now evident absurdity of the Stalinist experiment. Although still in transition, it is clear that Russia's only road to sanity is to reinstall market forces and to remove the economic wreckage left by Stalinism.

The planning done by our state highway departments and by the federal Department of Transportation (DOT) has much in common with that done by Gosplan. Decisions as to where and/or whether a highway is to be built in the United States depend on political and bureaucratic maneuvering, on pork barreling and on subsidies. These decisions are fully as arbitrary as the "planning" protocols of the old Gosplan system; realistic justifications are not part of the process.

Conclusions

There are now well over half a billion cars and trucks on the planet, over one for every ten humans. The world's car/truck population is growing at a rate two times that of the human population. In the United States there is one vehicle, car or truck, for every 1.4 humans; 36% (170 million in 1985) of all the vehicles on the planet are American. They are our major contributor to global warming, acid rain, ozone depletion and local air pollution. They also account for 45,000 deaths annually and hundreds of thousands of maimed and injured drivers, passengers and pedestrians.

American vehicles consume the equivalent of four billion barrels of oil each year, 20% of the world's oil production, half the motor fuel produced on the planet; each year they produce one billion tons of carbon dioxide, as well as vast amounts of nitrogen oxides and chlorofluorocarbons (CFCs), the major global warming gases. The rest of the world's cars and trucks produce only another billion tons of carbon dioxide, plus other gases. Compared to the contribution of American automobiles and trucks to global warming, the deplorable destruction of the world's rain forests is almost benign.

The verdict of the scientists on global warming is not yet fully confirmed, although it seems highly probable that the planet's climate will be significantly affected. Even if carbon dioxide, nitrous oxides and CFCs are exonerated, however, the cost of the impacts of the automobile, even the financial costs alone, is still too great for humanity, including (and particularly) Americans.

Obviously, market forces are not the only influences which affect our decisions; the automobile has intrinsic virtues and charms. Our need for status, authority and power are far more powerful than we will admit. For many transportation needs, the automobile is indispensable. However, environmental and economic abuse arise from the inevitable excess; rational individual decisions can be made by drivers only if we rectify the market forces which generate the unfortunate impacts of their overuse.

The elephant must be recognized; we must put aside denial. A level playing field must be provided between

2

DESTRUCTION AND REBUILDING OF PUBLIC TRANSPORTATION

"Only two infinities exist: the universe and the stupidity of the human race. I'm not certain about the former."
—Attributed to Albert Einstein

Public transportation, generally regarded as the inferior mode for getting where you want to go in the United States, is now comprised of publicly owned transit firms. These rely almost universally on diesel-powered buses. The firms are effectively bankrupt and survive only with the support of countervailing subsidies. The state of bankruptcy does not encourage delivery of attractive and effective service. This is the reality of present transit service in most American metropolitan centers. The only exceptions are the older, transit-oriented cities—New

York, San Francisco, Cleveland, Philadelphia, Chicago, Washington, DC—which furnish rail service.

Electric Rail Transit

The loss of electric railway transit in cities in the United States was accompanied by the concurrent losses of intercity freight and passenger railroad service. Buses, the dominant form of urban transit today, are vestiges of electric street railway systems that formerly served cities and towns throughout America. In many regions these areas also had electric interurban railway lines that served rural areas and provided fast, convenient passenger and freight services between cities. Streetcar and interurban services were the dominion of private firms that built and maintained their own infrastructure, paid taxes and received no subsidies.

The Conspiracy

Many believe that the loss of electric rail services and their replacement by buses is the result of a conspiracy by automotive interests which converted the nation into our existing automobile-dependency. This view is only partially true.

The conspiracy has been amply detailed in Congressional hearings and described in the media. Automobile manufacturers, oil, tire and related interests formed holding companies, like the National City Lines, and purchased street rail systems throughout the nation.

They then proceeded to junk the rail lines and vehicles and replace them with their own products—buses, tires and motor fuel. The converted firms, now buses only, were then spun off to become the orphaned charges of local governments.

The conspirators were tried and finally convicted in 1976; they were fined $5,000.

This tale of conspiracy is an attractive scapegoat; it permits us to believe that the auto, tire and oil industries are responsible for the disastrous loss of common carrier rail transport.

While condemnation of the automotive interests is richly deserved, the real villains are the collection of public policies which strongly favored the automobile over the streetcar resulting in the critical loss of transit patronage. The conspiracy was merely the coup de grace. Decades earlier industry had played a key role in promoting these policies.

The purpose of the conspirators was to increase the demand for their products. Further increases in demand for vehicles, tires and gasoline was achieved by pushing highways through the hearts of cities. The removal of streetcars and their replacement with diesel buses was accomplished during the 50s and 60s. With this change, the destruction of public transportation was assured. Concurrently the degradation of the central sections of large and mid-sized cities began in the nation.

The autos-roads-more-autos cycle became the routine; neighborhoods were destroyed, the sense of community was lost, suburban sprawl was encouraged. Decay of the inner cities and loss of civic pride resulted.

Public policy, at the same time that it was burdening trolley car and interurban railway firms with financial and other embarrassments, was creating a cost-free environment for the competing automobile. The motorist and the trucking industry were furnished huge subsidies in the form of free use of roadways, parking facilities and local government services. These subsidies and their effects, highly visible even before World War II, were the most important cause of the decline and bankruptcy of rail transit firms.

Roads for the use of buses were provided by local governments. Despite the pavement destruction created by the heavy buses, the roadways were maintained at public expense. Buses escaped the special taxes that were levied against street railways. Transit patrons immediately transferred to automobiles and to the new urban freeway system.

These conditions rapidly deteriorated; it became a world in which the streetcar business could not be profitable. The loss of patronage combined with punitive costs and special assessments on rail transit operators and their investors were decisive. The trolley car was doomed.

Substitution of buses for streetcars was the important goal of the automotive firms which formed the conspiracy. The myth that buses were superior, faster, more modern and comfortable was promulgated. The final trolley car run was often an occasion for parades and celebrations—"out with the old, in with the new"—following which the first buses roared off triumphantly in clouds of black diesel smoke.

Bus protagonists have argued that bus routes, being "flexible," could be extended and adjusted to meet changing travel patterns more cheaply and quickly than railways. However, the attractiveness of buses depends, in part, on the question of who pays the rent, repairs and maintenance cost for the infrastructure. If bus operators were required to pay rent and taxes for the highways occupied by their vehicles and if they were required to repair damaged pavement, they would see substantial increases in their expenses (and their subsidies).

The motor bus and its more attractive sibling, the trolley-bus, have their useful place. Under existing conditions, the combination of short bus and long rail lines is an optimal pattern making the best use of the strengths of each mode to provide efficient service in urban areas.

The Question of Population Density

Population density (the number of people/square mile) levels in the various American urban areas is regarded by some "experts" as the critical measure of viability for rail transit. These say that unless the area has Manhattan's population density, it cannot generate the patronage necessary for profitable operation of a rail transit system. They conclude that low-density cities must limit their choices of transportation modes to buses, carpools and single-occupant automobiles.

This is based on the assumption that public transit patrons comprise a fixed but very small percentage of the population. True believers are convinced that only urban corridors with high population densities within walking distance (one quarter of a mile) can generate farebox revenues sufficient to justify heavily capitalized rail lines.

Although bus levels of service are lower and operating costs are notably higher, they argue that capital investment and lead times to provide service are less. In support of this position, they cite Manhattan, Chicago and Washington, DC, where high population densities correlate with high transit patronage. Los Angeles and other American cities and their suburbs, said to have low population densities, are observed to have low transit ridership. This linkage makes the common error of an exchange of cause and effect. The true causal linkage is more complex. It leads to an entirely different conclusion.

Reality

Correlation between the foot size and reading ability of children does not prove that foot size is a reliable indicator of reading ability.

Foot size and a child's reading ability both increase with age; increasing age is much more believable as both cause and indicator of improvement in a child's reading ability. Evidently, tendencies to draw misleading conclusions from statistical correlations have not diminished with improved statistical methods. The correlation between density and patronage is misleading because the causal factors are more complex.

Population density has another quality; it correlates well with real estate values. High population densities mean high real estate values. Real estate in Manhattan is costly. Parking spaces are, therefore, hugely expensive. Free or validated parking is unthinkable.

Levels of patronage for rail transit and for taxis is high; subway transit patronage is high because free parking does not exist, *not* because population densities are high. Lower population densities result in lower property values; low property values permit employers and retail outlets to provide free or validated parking to attract employees and shoppers; free parking encourages automobile use; excessive levels of automobile use decimate transit patronage.

This causal chain is important to the transit debate. Los Angeles cannot be readily reconstructed to provide the Manhattan-like population densities said to be needed to meet this arbitrary density criteria. However, Los Angeles *can* reduce the availability of "free" and subsidized parking by careful reconstruction of its parking policies. By this means the community can favorably influence travel behavior, reduce traffic congestion, air pollution and increase transit patronage.

The Motor Bus and its Problems

Motor buses have many cost disadvantages compared to streetcars. They are labor intensive, particularly when amplified by low ridership levels. Real costs per passenger trip are high. Buses, not unlike automobiles and freeways, are characterized by both economies and diseconomies of scale. When patronage levels increase, costs per passenger trip first decrease then increase as vehicle densities increase. When automobile use increases, the same phenomenon occurs. Apart from their ability to use existing roadways, motor buses are neither attractive nor efficient.

Buses last about 12 years; rail cars three or four times as long. The cost of buses must also include that of maintaining pavements. Buses axle loads are as heavy as those of 18-wheel trucks; urban pavements are quickly destroyed. Buses run on urban streets and arterials; they increase congestion. They are slower than automotive traffic because they must stop to load and off-load passengers.

Bus schedules are notoriously difficult to maintain on longer routes because of frequent stops and the joint use of streets. Schedule deviations increase with bus route length; the longer the route, the greater the deviation.

The use of buses on long routes (say, over five miles in length) does not permit effective coordination of intersecting routes. Coordination is critical if the area is to be served with grid-like route systems and provided with acceptable levels of service. Short lines are more tractable with regard to schedules.

The Effects of Sprawl

The evolution of urban patterns in the 30s into suburban-sprawl had serious consequences for transit; residential areas moved beyond existing trolley lines. Those unable to drive were unable to hold their jobs when employers migrated from the central city.

In his study of the impacts of the automobile on Atlanta from 1900 to 1935, Howard L. Preston concludes that since ". . . whites could generally better afford the price of an automobile, it gave them a novel advantage over black Atlantans: greater mobility and an opportunity to act out their racist views by moving away to planned suburban neighborhoods on the north side."

The consequences of middle-class "white flight" contributed to the suburbanization of American cities. The American street railway was another victim of this phenomenon; its demise increased American dependence on the automobile and, thereby, reduced constraints on sprawl.

Discriminatory Regulation of Street Railways

Street railways were owned and financed by private firms. The firms constructed and maintained their own infrastructure, paid taxes and, in many cases, discriminatory special fees. Many cities, for example, required that they repair and maintain the pavement between their rails plus a specified distance (usually two feet) on either side. In addition, they removed snow and paid part of the cost of bridges along their routes, even those required by competing automobiles.

Although vigorous competition was furnished by the personal automobile and by jitneys and taxicabs, the rail firms were regarded as though they were monopolies not unlike gas, water and electric utilities. Agencies of state and local governments regulated fare levels, safety, labor practices and equipment.

In many urban areas in the United States, electric street railway service was provided by the local electric utility company. This marriage of convenience was both logical and fortuitous. The same crews could maintain the power systems of both businesses. Many of the same skills were needed for equipment maintenance on utility and street railway properties. The trolley car firms furnished efficient, quality transit service in many mid-size American cities.

The federal government, pursuing antitrust policies, forced power companies that owned street railways to divest themselves of their transit operations. As an antitrust action this is difficult to understand. Although both power and traction companies were natural monopolies, they provided widely different services; joint ownership was a natural partnership. The antitrust prosecution was a serious blow to electric railway systems.

Safety requirements were discriminatory as compared to the automotive competition. New York State laws require that streetcars be equipped with a "deadman's control" which would bring the car to a halt if the operator is incapacitated. The cars were equipped with safety fenders or cow-catchers to protect pedestrians from being caught beneath the wheels. Doors were interlocked with the brakes to prevent the car from moving with the doors open.

As useful as these provisions are, similar ones were not imposed on buses. In some areas, city regulations required the use of two-person crews on streetcars, but not on buses. Fares were regulated even though street railways, staggering from patronage loss to the personal automobile, were unable to exploit a monopolistic advantage.

The President's Conference Committee (PCC)

In the face of these afflictions, the street railway industry did not surrender easily; it made a last attempt to avoid destruction. During the 1930s, the presidents of American street railway firms met to consider their deteriorating situation. Conscious of the potential efficiencies of the street railways and aware, also, of their large investment in tracks and power distribution facilities, they found that current streetcars, although sturdy, were obsolete. The "Presidents' Conference Committee" (PCC) was formed, charged with design of a modern streetcar.

When the first PCC cars were unveiled in the late 1930s, they were an instant success; they were fast, their acceleration was better than that of most automobiles. Handsome, comfortable and quiet, these new streetcars had been carefully designed, incorporating the best technical standards. Large fleets went into service in nearly every American city. Where the tracks were located on reserved rights-of-way, the PCC cars ran at speeds approaching those of rapid transit trains providing levels of service significantly higher than that of buses.

World War II restricted driving; shortages of gasoline, oil, vehicles and tires increased streetcars patronage. The newly modernized street railways did faithful duty, but the war's end removed these restraints. Automobile and highway interests prevailed with the aid of the automotive conspiracy. Buses took over.

Conclusion

By the early 1950s, the number of cities that still had significant streetcar companies were a pitiful few. With the end of streetcars the transit companies, now depending on motor buses, lost even more patronage. This decline can be attributed, in part, to reduced service provided by buses. Increasing automobile ownership and subsidized driving was, of course, the major reason.

Then followed a precipitous withdrawal of private capital from transit systems. The flight of capital, of course, signaled the end of privately owned transit firms and the end of the street railway systems.

Bankrupt and cast loose by the conspiracy that had destroyed them, the transit firms could not be allowed to die. A significant portion of the citizenry—the poor, the disabled, the young and the old, those who cannot afford or are unable to operate automobiles—are dependent on public transit service. Like abandoned wives and children, transit firms found themselves on the doorsteps of city and county governments throughout the nation.

They were and are unwelcome wards because, as political leaders and taxpayers soon learned, circumstances made bus transit a financial black-hole. Farebox revenues notoriously fail to meet operating needs. Large subsidies must be provided to keep the still essential bus firms in business, even at wholly inadequate service levels. This absurdity can be traced to the irrational policies which still bedevil American commuters and their alter egos, American taxpayers.

With the end of public transportation came the demise of the domestic railcar building industry that had furnished the nation's needs and had exported electric rail equipment throughout the world. The loss of the industry dispersed the cadre of specialists and caused the loss of their design, building and operating skills.

These losses have not been replaced. Recently when Americans, fed up with gridlocked traffic and air pollution, began to demand street railways, they found that railway cars, as well as the necessary skills to make them had to be imported from nations that had, in the intervening years, retained and upgraded their railway transit systems.

Intercity rail passenger service, provided until the 50s by privately operated railroad firms, is now the responsibility of Amtrak, a federal agency which depends heavily upon taxpayer subsidies. It also functions currently at comparatively low levels of service. This is improving steadily as patronage improves and as the public begins to experience once again the advantages of rail travel.

Reconstruction of street railways has begun. Projects have been completed in many cities. Patronage and public acceptance have often exceeded expectations.

Critics have argued that the cost per trip is too high; this is disingenuous. Transit is characterized by economies of scale; the more patronage, the less expensive the trip. Rail transit is potentially far less costly than automobiles, freeways or buses.

The nation must establish higher priorities for rebuilding urban rail transit. The marketplace distortions which created the problem must be corrected. The public will learn that patronage will be more than adequate to justify these investments.

3

THE COSTS OF SPACE

"Prices perform three functions in organizing economic activity; first, they transmit information; second, they provide an incentive to adopt those methods of production that are least costly and, thereby, use available resources for the most highly valued purposes; third, they determine who gets how much of the product—the distribution of income. These three functions are closely interrelated." —Milton Friedman, *Free to Choose*

There are two important aspects of the automobile-dependent society which have attracted little attention: first, it needs costly space. And, secondly, space is usually free to the motorist, although it is a major expense to the community. Planning authorities and politicians pander to the automobile. They make every effort to see that its need for space is satisfied, even sated.

The failure to collect rents for highway and parking facilities, enormously costly resources to both the public and private sectors, is the most important determinant in the critical modal choices made by American travellers. Custom seems to be the only basis for the practice of furnishing free use of parking and highways.

Custom, as we have learned in recent years, can be changed. At present, it is reinforced because of the needs of retail stores to attract shoppers (parking is essential), the needs of cities (whose interest is in the collection of maximum sales tax revenues) and the needs of employers in obtaining competent staff.

The use of parking and highway facilities is widely regarded as a "public good"; this perception is often used to justify the provision of their use free to the user. But free use is not the defining characteristic of a public good. Public goods are those that, having been enjoyed by the consumer, are not consumed but remain to be enjoyed by other consumers. The consumption of these goods does not destroy them. Examples are public parks, the national defense, radio and television broadcasts.

The user of public goods should, where possible and appropriate, bear the cost. In the case of public parks, the community believes that it is in the public interest to provide their use free to the user. The national defense, by its nature, cannot be charged to the individual on the basis of its use, it must be paid for, like the public parks, by a tax on all citizens—all citizens receive the benefits. Television and radio broadcasts, because of their nature, cannot be charged for except on a voluntary basis, as in public radio and the public broadcasting system.

Highway and parking facilities are public goods (although, strictly speaking, their use by motorists or truck drivers reduces their utility for others—motorists, pedestrians and bicyclists); they can be paid for as a condition of use. Privately operated parking lots, toll highways and toll bridges demonstrate that these facilities need not be "free" goods. Highways and parking are free goods because of custom and the desire of retail businesses and employers to gain or to maintain a competitive advantage.

Free use of costly space is the equivalent of a subsidy to the driver. Subsidies generate excessive use. But automobiles and trucks are seen as desirable and beneficial. Can we have too much of a good thing?

Parking

As we were being seated, I remarked that the motorists who had used the restaurant's parking lot would not pay for parking. My friend, an economics professor and pedant to the core, instructed me: "Of course they will pay. Our bill for lunch will include an increment sufficient to cover the cost of rent for this restaurant. That increment will be increased by a portion for the parking spaces. Otherwise, the restaurateur and the landlord could not stay in business."

"But," I said, with satisfaction, "we walked here."

Subsidized driving is not the only effect of "free" parking; inequity is another. Parking, of course, is not free. And the question of who paid is not trivial. The parking portion of the rental increment (and of our luncheon bill) was not insignificant.

At real estate values of $660,000 per acre (probably conservative) and assuming there were 150 parking spaces per acre, at ten percent interest plus the cost of paving, striping and maintenance the rental cost of one use of each space, assuming five uses per day, for one and a half hours per use, with the lot 70% full, was almost 40¢. Our luncheon bills came to about five dollars. The parking spaces, which we had not used, had increased our luncheon bills by almost nine percent. But this was Orange County and land was relatively cheap.

For employers, the costs are similar. For locations closer to the center of the city, rents are higher; land is more expensive. Each space is used once per day for 250 days per year; the market cost per space is perhaps twelve dollars per day ($250 per month). Assuming an average salary of $35,000, the cost of parking increases payroll expense by 8.6%. Furthermore, since the expense to the employer of providing parking for employees is fully deductible (and the benefit to the employee is not counted as income), "free" parking increases the tax burden for all Americans.

The free use of parking spaces makes driving irresistibly cheap. Not surprisingly, the commuter's modal choice is heavily affected by the level of parking subsidy provided by his employer. Several academic studies, virtually all originating with the virtuoso of parking, Professor Don Shoup (UCLA), have demonstrated that parking subsidies are the most important determinant of modal choice. The most recent of these, *The Effects of Employer-Paid Parking in Downtown Los Angeles: A*

Study of Office Workers and Their Employers (Willson and Shoup, May 1990), shows that over two and a half times as many commuters in the Los Angeles Central Business District (CBD) use transit to commute if their employers do *not* subsidize parking. These figures correlate well with several other studies.

The figure reported by the Willson/Shoup paper is probably low for the Los Angeles area. The Central Business District is a special case: it is the area of Los Angeles best-served by the bus system. Carpooling and vanpooling, for the same reasons, are most possible in the CBD. Market prices for parking in the CBD are much higher than in other parts of Los Angeles. Parking is more visible and available in other parts of the city. While there is little or no data for other parts of Los Angeles (or for other cities), single-occupant car-commuting is even more prevalent in non-central city areas. Although market prices for parking outside the CBD are less, subsidized parking is still an important determinant for driving; furthermore, transit service and carpooling are not as attractive as in the CBD.

Federal and state tax policies contribute to this situation. The marginal tax rate for corporations is over 50%; the cost of employee parking is a deductible cost of doing business. Subsidized parking is an attractive option for the employer; it provides a low-cost tax-free benefit to the employee (the equivalent, added to the salary in cash, would require that the employee pay a substantial tax on the increase).

IRS regulations are relevant: the IRS permits employer-furnished transportation allowances of $15 monthly paid in cash or equivalent (say, a transit pass). The employee is not required to declare this as income. If the employer is more generous—let us say that the employer-furnished allowance is $15.01 or more—the entire amount must be declared. Monthly bus passes priced at $15 or less are rare indeed; they are generally $40 or more.

Retail businesses and employers furnish subsidized parking because they must compete for employees and clients. The consequence is that frivolous, as well as necessary, trips are made by personal automobile.

Trips by bus transit in Los Angeles are only two to four percent of all trips in the area. This inadequate level of demand has destroyed the rail transit systems; the bus systems operate with heavy losses and abysmal levels of service. Los Angelenos who can afford them thus opt for their personal automobiles.

All working adults in Los Angeles are virtually required to own an automobile and to use it for all trips. The expense of maintaining and operating the vehicles, now accepted as a legitimate part of the cost of living, is added to labor's demands for a living wage.

Thus, the cost of owning a car and the cost of driving, plus the cost of highway and parking facilities, are passed through as additions to the cost of American products. This is a cost/price disadvantage which does not handicap our more efficient competitors. Citizens of Japan, Germany, Taiwan and Korea are not automobile dependent.

The level of service perceived by each motorist is determined by the availability of space in parking facilities as well as on highways. The vehicles are in storage about 95% of their lifetime, so that parking may be the more important of the two automotive uses of urban space.

Our observations in Los Angeles lead us to believe that, at present levels of service (convenience), each vehicle requires eight parking spaces—one full-use space at home, one at work, the remainder in fractional-use spaces at supermarkets, retail stores, doctors, dentists, restaurants and other business establishments throughout the city.

If more vehicles are brought into the community without increasing the number of parking spaces, the level of service will decline and it becomes more difficult for the motorist to find a parking space at more places in the city.

Plagued by "spill-over" parking in front of their homes, householders press politicians and planners to increase the requirements for building code parking spaces. Local government planners use their building permit authority to demand more and more parking capacity for newly constructed buildings. Politicians and planners are convinced that, by requiring this excessive parking capacity, they are increasing the public good at the expense of the builder. In some cases in Los Angeles, as the ultimate weapon in their battle against spill-over parking, planners have ruled (with the support of the law) that parking fees may not be charged for these spaces.

That there is no cost for parking is, as we have seen, a myth. Parking requirements enormously increase the cost of American buildings. In the absence of parking fees, these costs are passed through to the consumer, willy nilly, via increased rents and increased prices for products. This is one of the several important reasons why American manufacturing jobs have flown overseas to more hospitable shores.

At first blush, eight parking spaces appear to be a surprisingly large number of spaces required for the average vehicle. The magnitude seems reasonable, however, because it correlates well with the assessments of other observers of the urban space allotted to the automobile. Motorist convenience demands empty spaces.

Eight spaces, assuming they are all "asphalt" spaces, require at least 2,000 square feet of urban real estate. If they are provided in structures, less real estate is required, but each space is far more expensive because of the cost of the structures. 2,000 square feet is about 1/20th of an acre. Urban acres are expensive; for our purposes we will assume a valuation of $200,000 per acre. At an interest rate of ten percent, 1/20th of an acre should demand a minimum annual rental of about $1,000. To be conservative, we have purposely ignored the cost of structures, paving, striping, maintenance (sweeping and repair) and other costs such as wages for attendants, etc.

This is a rough approximation; data is lacking. Although it is an estimate, it is clearly a lower-bound figure and it demonstrates that the cost of parking is an important, not a trivial component of the cost of living.

Highways

The principle of charging rent for the use of highways is not easy to defend. American custom regards the use of highways as "free" goods. Highway facilities are not only public property, the investment in highways is a "sunk" cost; highways are not going to be plowed and planted to asparagus, even if and when they are unneeded as highways.

The investment made in the past by the community ought to return a benefit to the whole community, not only to the motorist. The driver gets the free use of this huge investment at the same time that similar investments (say, in residential and commercial buildings) are paid for only by those who benefit from their use, not by the entire community.

Children, living in their parents' home, pay no rent. The community, which owns the roads, is not the parent of the motorist. The affectionate ties between parents and children which permit children to live rent-free should not, exist between society and its members.

That relationship should properly be a business relationship, constrained by the normal rules of doing business. In fact, that is a rule that governs all transactions between citizen and society with the exception of the rules pertaining to public welfare. Highways should not remain in that category.

Our estimate of the cost of necessary vehicle space on highways is as simple as our calculation of the cost of necessary parking space. Most traffic lanes are twelve feet wide; the average car probably travels (for our purposes) at 35 mph. If we assume that each motorist on the freeway permits a headway of one car-length for each ten mph, then the space for each vehicle in full flight on the freeway is $4\frac{1}{2}$ x 17 x 12 = 918 square feet. If we now accept that our motorist requires an additional operating space on roadways and arterials equal to this, we approach 2,000 square feet.

Applying costing factors similar to our parking calculation, we determine that the rental cost for highways is roughly $1,000 per year per vehicle. Remember that we have not included the cost of construction which should, at least, double the figure. Thus, we can again say that our figures are a lower bound.

It is argued that highways are necessary to provide access to dwellings and businesses; therefore, the owners and users of the property are legitimately charged with this expense by means of property and sales taxes. Even if automobiles were not generally used, this argument goes, it would still be necessary to deliver goods (furniture, building materials, etc.), pick up garbage, provide access for police cars, fire trucks, and for emergency vehicles.

While such access is necessary, are the roadways and arterials properly designed for this public service access?

Minimum roadways in residential neighborhoods are commonly 40 feet curb to curb (two twelve-foot lanes plus two eight-foot parking lanes); twelve-foot parkways, including four-foot sidewalks are also required—a 64 foot right-of-way. Arterials: four or six twelve-foot lanes plus two eight-foot parking lanes (64 or 78 foot curb to curb) plus center strips, left-turn pockets, plus mandatory sidewalks, perhaps parkways—at least 84, possibly 120 feet.

There are existing communities in the United States that do not permit the use of automobiles; the occupants of these communities have the need to provide access for vehicles for garbage collection, police and fire protection. These communities are our college and university campuses; they function universally with far less expensive roadways.

The common usage on campus is a twelve-foot-wide roadway which furnishes sufficient, effective access for all purposes. Students, faculty and staff use their legs and bicycles to get from building to building. Public service vehicles use the roadways without difficulty. Forty foot roadways are unnecessary on campuses, much less 64 or 88 foot widths, to provide for garbage collection, police and fire protection or furniture moving.

The example of campus roadways demonstrates that the 40-foot or greater width roadway is not required to provide access for public service vehicles but, rather, such wide roadways are required for access and storage of personal automobiles in large numbers. The cost of the campus version of a roadway network is negligible compared to the cost of the roadways required for universal automobile use.

Taxation of Highway Right-of-Way

Where land is devoted to any purpose, the direct beneficiary should, like the beneficiaries of the use of other property, be required to pay property taxes for the support of community services. The property taxes paid by the nation's privately-owned railroads on their rights-of-way, for instance, were at one time among the largest sources of funds for a number of local governments. The users of the nation's highways, in contrast, pay no taxes at all on the much greater area of rights-of-way which they occupy.

Highway protagonists will argue that the highway right-of-way, being publicly owned, is accessible to all; that the railroad right-of-way is privately owned. Is the railroad or the highway the most publicly accessible? Travellers using the highway must possess automobiles or trucks; to use the railroad, they need only purchase a ticket.

Conclusion

The cost of parking is subsumed in the cost of products and it is clearly a substantial part, probably four to five percent, of the nation's GNP. The cost of highways is similar in both magnitude and principle; however, it is not now counted as a portion of the GNP. In our opinion it should be. It amounts to another four to five percent.

This eight to ten percent of the GNP could be more usefully spent in increasing the productivity of the nation. Instead, it is used to induce excessive use of our automobiles, the most costly and the most wasteful mode of urban transportation.

4

LOCAL GOVERNMENT:
PROPOSITION 13 AND THE TAX REVOLT

"... They're throwing money out of City Hall windows ..."
—slogan used in Howard Jarvis' campaign for Proposition 13

In 1978, the California Proposition 13 campaign was led by Howard Jarvis, an articulate Los Angeles curmudgeon whose message was that local government bungling, waste and corruption were the cause of the steep property tax increases which had occurred during the several preceding years. Property tax foreclosures had hit the front pages and the Jarvis message found an interested audience of California homeowners; they were terrified.

Jarvis' claims were wild distortions, although they contained partial truths. The tax system *was* badly tilted against California homeowners. Unfortunately, Jarvis' Proposition 13 was designed to correct the symptom, not the illness. The problem, like an insect trapped in amber, remains embedded in the state tax system, still creating mischief. The nation's taxpayers believe, naively, that tax levels are adjusted so as to be appropriate to the various costs incurred by government. With regard to the gas tax and the property tax, nothing could be further from the truth. The relationship of the two intertwined taxes is critical to an understanding of the origins of California's Proposition 13.

Local (city and county) governments in the United States are complex and unique. They provide virtually all police and fire protection, street repair, traffic control, parks, urban planning and myriad other services which directly impact the welfare of all citizens. Other specialized local agencies furnish public education, library services, water supply and, occasionally, other utilities.

Voters often take local government for granted—witness the very low turnout at elections. This reflects apathy or, possibly, occasional satisfaction with the quiet functioning of these complicated institutions.

Despite its low profile, local government is responsible for huge expenditures. The aggregate of the annual expenditures of 82,000 nationwide local governmental entities exceeds $500 billion—ten percent of the nation's gross national product. This exceeds an average of $5,000 for every household in the nation.

Local government, of course, meets important needs— police and fire protection, roads, schools, flood control, sewers, courts, emergency medical aid. It is a mainstay of our democratic traditions. Local officials are intimately involved in dealing with the needs of their constituents.

They are immediately available (sometimes painfully so) to occasionally indignant voter-taxpayers.

Local governments are supported by various combinations of taxes. Property and sales taxes are virtually universal. The combined yields of these two taxes comprise, nationwide, the major portion of local government income.

In California, as in many other states, fuel taxes are collected by the state government. While the practice varies among the states, the rates of the sales tax, the fuel tax and the in-lieu tax (auto license fee) are established by the legislature. The state remits portions (roughly half) of the yield of these taxes to its cities and counties.

The yield of the fuel tax and the in-lieu tax once constituted substantial portions of city and county incomes and budgets but in California as in most states, the legislature failed to increase these two taxes despite inflationay reduction in yield. This refusal was probably due to the belief that taxpayers would be less indignant if the sales tax were increased (the yield from a one percent increase in the sales tax roughly equals a ten cents per gallon increase in the fuel tax). So, instead, sales taxes were increased.

The property tax rate is established by local government and is the only major tax in California actually assessed and collected by local government.

The failure to keep fuel taxes in line with inflation created large imbalances in local government budgets in the 60s and 70s. Property tax increases, the result of inflation-driven real estate values and the resulting foreclosures before the June 1978 election, were the result of this imbalance and of the convergence of several trends and practices, some peculiar to California:

- The relative importance, in the early 60s, of gasoline tax and in-lieu tax revenues to city and county budgets.
- The failure of the legislature to increase the gasoline and in-lieu taxes to keep pace with inflation.
- The steep inflation, beginning in the early 60s, which eventually multiplied all costs including government costs by a factor of three (now four).
- Even steeper inflation in real estate values in the 60s and 70s.
- The practice, at least in one county, of reassessing real property only at four or five year intervals.

The gasoline tax is a gallonage tax. Although the human population of the state increased from 1965 to 1984, the population of cars and trucks increased at a more rapid rate; the vehicle miles travelled (VMT) increased at an even greater rate. Thus, gasoline consumption remained roughly constant during the period, possibly because of federally imposed Corporate Automotive Fuel Efficiency (CAFE) standards. Cars became smaller and more efficient and could travel many more miles per gallon of gasoline.

Consequently, in adjusted dollars, fuel tax and license fee revenues decreased rapidly with inflation. The resulting shortfall was fortuitously filled by the increased yield from the property tax.

But the increase in the property tax bills fell on only a few unfortunate homeowners whose property had been reassessed at the wrong time. Those who could not pay their suddenly swollen tax bills lost their property. The press took notice. Homeowners were frightened by the headlines, Jarvis stoked the panic with exaggerated allegations of waste and corruption. The rest is history.

City and county governments provide virtually all highway and parking infrastructure and services essential to motorists and to the trucking industry. Exceptions are state and federal highways and privately provided parking facilities.

Cities and counties furnish traffic signals, traffic engineering services, police and fire protection for motorists, traffic control, auto theft control, street lighting, street repair and maintenance, flood control, parking facilities, paramedics, courts, hospitals, air pollution control and related services.

Since the aggregate of these services is a major category of municipal expense, the natural question is: "Do those who benefit (motorists and the trucking industry) pay enough in taxes to reimburse our city and county governments for these expenditures?"

Obviously, they do not. For every dollar motorists pay to local governments, the governments spend eight dollars to provide them with these essential services.

Equity is severely abused, but that is not the only impact. Market forces which determine the level of automotive vehicle use are distorted by the effects of this shortfall. Combined with the underpricing of parking and the use of highways, the shortfalls guarantee excessive use of our highway system. They create enormous inefficiencies as well as the destruction of our public transit infrastructure.

The next question is: "Does a mechanism exist which adjusts the motorist and trucker-paid taxes to the level of the related costs of State, city and county governments?"

The answer is "no." Or, more exactly, the state legislature, which should adjust these taxes, does not do so. To be even more exact, it is evident that neither the legislature nor any other authority believes that it has this responsibility. The allocation of costs among the motorists, the trucking industry and the community is left to industry lobbyists and the luck of the draw.

The highly organized and powerful automotive interests—auto clubs, trucking associations, auto manufacturers, oil industry, highway contractors and state highway departments—have been diligent and effective in preventing this needed adjustment. They have become rich and powerful by effectively expanding and protecting their markets.

Whereas in 1965 state remissions from the fuel tax and the in-lieu tax comprised about one-half of California local government automobile-related costs, inflation had reduced this to about one-eighth of such costs by 1984.

The value of this shortfall in 1985 was the equivalent of 40 to 50¢ per gallon at current rates of consumption. Aggregated nationwide, this would amount to $60 billion annually (which by 1988 was more than twice the value of national farm subsidies or somewhat more than the total national welfare budget).

These same local governments contend daily with the twin problems of traffic congestion and air pollution. In pursuit of better air quality the Southern California Air Quality Management District (SCAQMD) attempts to decrease automotive trips.

Its efforts now utilize a bureaucratic command strategy: the SCAQMD has promulgated Regulation XV which requires businesses employing 100 or more employees at a single location to provide incentives to drive less in commuting.

Other SCAQMD efforts attempt to impact local government planning, requiring an increase in the "jobs/housing balance" which states that jobs shall be provided where housing is and housing where jobs are.

Question: "Will these command strategies work when existing economic incentives are pressing powerfully in the opposite direction?" The answer is "Of course not."

Two-thirds of municipal budgets, nationwide, are derived from property and sales tax yields. All individuals, whether they own or rent, pay both taxes. The poor pay proportionately more of these taxes from their smaller incomes. Local government budget shortfalls derived from expenditures for motorist-related needs are balanced, inevitably, by the yield from these two regressive taxes.

The case of Yonkers, NY is instructive. In the 1940s Yonkers was a prosperous city of 150,000. Highly industrialized, it was the base for Otis Elevator, Habirshaw Wire & Cable and Alexander Shaw Carpets, among others. The city's largest property taxpayer was the New York Central Railroad.

During the 1950s the New York Thruway was built, passing through the city taking in its path 700 pieces of Yonkers real estate, removing them from the property tax rolls. The Thruway, though a toll highway, pays no property taxes. The other property taxpayers, of necessity, had to pick up the burden of this increment.

Since the Thruway was built, Otis Elevator, Habirshaw Wire & Cable and Alexander Shaw Carpets have moved to other cities (not entirely because of the effects of the New York Thruway, of course). Because its patronage was diverted to motoring and trucking on the Thruway, the New York Central was bankrupted, its property tax contributions lost to local government. It has been taken over by Conrail and by Metro North commuter services, both of which must be publicly supported.

Similarly, Pasadena, in the mid-70s, lost ten percent of its property tax rolls because of the construction of the Route 210 Freeway which sliced through the city's heart, carrying much of its retail trade to neighboring cities.

San Jose's central city features two freeway interchanges which, alone, occupy a total of 200 acres. Four freeways absorb hundreds of more acres. San Jose real estate taxes which would normally have been collected on this huge acreage have also been lost to San Jose citizens.

The Yonkers, Pasadena and San Jose experiences have been duplicated in a thousand other American cities. Highway engineers are not concerned with local governments and the sources of the tax yields which support their budgets.

Shortfalls

Local government shortfalls constitute de facto subsidies encouraging drivers to use their cars in commuting and in other trips. Since single-occupant automobiles compete with mass transit in the same marketplace, this subsidy helps destroy mass transit patronage. Other subsidies, like the free use of parking and highway facilities are even more important economic pressures.

American public transit firms are now in local government ownership supported by large public subsidies. De facto subsidies create an important side-effect: the necessity of supporting public transit with countervailing subsidies in order to keep the buses running at all. For Los Angeles County, the aggregate of transit subsidies is now over $400 million or about $50 per year, per inhabitant.

In order to minimize the huge transit subsidies, low service levels are the norm. Bus headways are lengthy, long waits at the bus stop are the rule; routes are long and schedules unreliable. The local truism is that it takes two hours to go anywhere by bus. Thus the non-driving poor are confined to their ghettoes, effectively separated from jobs and other amenities of urban life.

This is fiscal absurdity. Citizens in their roles as wage-earners, consumers and taxpayers are required to support two subsidies: the first being a huge de facto subsidy to drivers. The second is paid to the transit system to offset the egregious effects of the first.

The consequence of both subsidies is to create two costly and highly unsatisfactory transportation systems. Those who suffer from the disease, incredibly, are required to pay to sustain it. The burden of increased prices and taxes is not only an unnecessary injury to everyone but is a basic cause of urban degradation in the nation.

While Proposition 13 has provided some benefits to some taxpayers, it has also created great inequities. Yet the Proposition and its myth are still with us, creating many problems for Californians. Neighbors may pay wildly differing property taxes since property is permitted to be reassessed only upon changes in ownership. Homeowners now question the wisdom and the inequities imposed by Proposition 13.

The failure to provide an equitable balance between the fuel tax and the property tax has created unfair benefits to motorists and to the trucking industry with the subsidies paid by property and sales taxes and through retail prices and paychecks. The diversion of property tax funds, plus the provisions of Proposition 13, has had serious consequences. It results in understaffed police and fire departments and underfunded schools, parks and libraries.

Perhaps that is what the voters want. We doubt it. One thing *is* certain; the basic causes of the pre-1978 problems are still there.

So are the problems.

5

BEHAVIORAL PATTERNS
All Hat, No Cows

"If you're anxious for to shine in the high aesthetic line as a
man of culture rare,
You must get up all the germs of transcendental terms, and
plant them everywhere,
You must lie upon the daisies and discourse in novel phrases of
your complicated state of mind,
The meaning doesn't matter if it's only idle chatter of a
transcendental kind.
    And every one will say,
    As you walk your mystic way,
'If this young man expresses himself in terms too deep for me,
'Why, what a very singularly deep young man this deep young
man must be!' "

        —"Bunthorne's Song," *Patience*, Gilbert and Sullivan

Having satisfied their needs for food, shelter, and sex,
people's next task is to establish themselves as powerful
both in their own eyes and in the eyes of society. This

longing for self-esteem, recognition and dignity probably has a relationship to the compulsion to make war and to exploit one's neighbors.

The leaders of the auto industry have not lost sight of this peculiarity of its market. They know which buttons to push; they do not misjudge market fundamentals:

- *"Your job is a 7½. Your relationship is an 8. Shouldn't your car be a 10?"*
  —An advertisement for the Infiniti (Nissan)

- *"Emerge victorious instead of victimized—The Ultimate Driving Machine!"*
  —Caption on a billboard showing a racy sedan leaving a freeway—an advertisement for BMWs.

"Where is the morality in deliberately designing an automobile to meet some defect in a customer's character? . . . Are you saying that your new car customers are nitwits? . . . That your new car is not primarily a means of transportation? . . . That it is some abstraction to bemuse a [person] who thinks a machine can be more than a machine?"
—John Keats, *Insolent Chariots*, 1967

Let us admit that the search for recognition does not yield to the ordinary economic behavior analysis; further-more, economist-theorists are not fond of the subject. Young men are risk-takers, a fact attested to by automobile insurance rates. When not seeking glory in the cannon's mouth, young men choose racy automobiles and careers, tailgating and slaloming on the freeway on the way to work. Not quite the cannon's mouth, but second-best macho is better than none.

Porsches, Corvettes and other muscle cars are usually the choice of young men; for older men—and women—also prone to ego-enhancement and status-seeking, the choice is often the also expensive, but staid sedan—BMW, Mercedes Benz or Infiniti.

While a necessity for transportation, cars are also status symbols and ego-enhancers. There are varying proportions of both pizzazz and utility in all automobiles. "Performance," "comfort," "quality," "fine" or "luxury" are jargon routinely used to conceal this reality. There are metaphors in the animal kingdom which would seem to establish these tendencies as gene-related. One example are two tropical bird species living in close proximity in the rain forest—the Manucode and the Raggiana.

Raggiana are Birds of Paradise; the males are splendid. Raggiana males employ dramatic gestures in courtship; after courting and mating, they pursue other females. The females raise the young by themselves. Raggiana diets are rich in protein; they prefer insects. Small catches suffice; the males devote leisure time to courtship.

In contrast, Manucode feathers are drab and unpretentious. Manucode courtship is more subdued; they live on fruit, a far less satisfying diet, requiring much time and work to harvest. Both male and female must work full time to feed their young. The contrast in the breeding habits of the two species is believed to have evolved in correlation with and because of their respective diets.

American courtship practices are analogous to that of the Raggiana: rich young men employ big, dramatic automobiles. Much money is spent on macho devices and behavior.

The Cadillac Syndrome

Why do people buy Cadillacs? One might claim they provide more comfort; but it would seem that the small margin of comfort compared to that of less costly competing vehicles implies there is something involved other than comfort.

If we label adequate comfort a "hard" utility and status or ego-satisfaction a "soft" utility we would discover that soft utilities do not follow the normal demand/supply curve. When the price is increased, demand not infrequently goes up, not down. Demand does not decrease as rapidly with price increases as do other, harder utilities.

For those who pursue status and ego-satisfaction, price has its own utility. The high price confers status and greater gratification to those whose needs are satisfied.

Irrational? Perhaps. Whatever the case, we observe that there are a lot of irrational consumers out there.

Middle-class attitudes with regard to lawns and flowers, particularly in the front of the house, is another aspect of the need for identification and status as a member of the middle class. Clothes, used like uniforms, also establish identity and status. Religion, for some believers, satisfies the same need.

Luxury automobiles are conspicuous consumption. A substantial portion of their total utility, however, is transportation. This confers a legitimacy that diamonds cannot. Furthermore, spending too much money on automobiles is not criminal; buyers may do as they like with their money.

In addition to questionable taste, however, large, expensive automobiles do two things that are antithetical to the public interest. They unnecessarily divert funds from the investment stream into non-productive use, thereby abusing the public interest. Secondly, they excessively consume energy and space, both of which have claims to public property rights (rights not defined in the law). Whether or not our philosophy provodes derision, disapproval is based on a foundation of reason, it is thus a matter which ought, for obvious reasons, to be on the public agenda.

The cost of providing the "soft" utility is certainly very large for the United States. There are more BMWs, Mercedes and Rolls Royces in Beverly Hills than in Germany and England. The amount of capital spent on soft utility is, effectively, economic waste, even though it represents a utility for the purchasers of such vehicles.

Conspicuous consumption attempts to achieve status by conferring elegance on the consumer. It may actually succeed; Gucci shoes, Brooks Brothers suits, Eddie Bauer or REI sweaters. Elegance is in the eye of the beholder.

Much of the money spent on automobiles to establish an image of elegance—expensive cars, roll-bars, flood lights, "spoilers," racing stripes, the snoods used to protect the front ends of sporty models, the eyebrows now installed on windshield wipers, the stuffed animals positioned upside-down on the inside of car windows—has the opposite effect.

The prostitute's garish dress, the gaudy automobile, the Rolex watch or the pinky ring of a drug dealer, or the stretch limousine and mauve tuxedo of a high school prom, also examples of conspicuous consumption, are not elegance measured against any reasonable standard. Quite the contrary.

Impacts

Oil is a fungible commodity; oil is traded on a worldwide market. Additional demand for oil in any part of the world will increase the price. Increased supplies of oil from any part of the world will send the price downward.

Luxury automobiles, because they are larger and heavier, are gas guzzlers compared to cars which provide only the hard utilities—adequate comfort, reliability, safety and transportation. Consuming more gasoline than is necessary to provide the hard utilities, luxury cars increase the world price of oil. This has several important results:

- By increasing the price of oil world-wide, the price of kerosene bought by peasants of the third world is also increased. Kerosene is use as a substitute for wood for cooking and for light. Thus, BMWs, Mercedes and Cadillacs increase the financial burdens borne by the poorest of humanity. Deforestation is also increased.

- More money is put into the pockets of the oil industry, as well as into those of the Kuwaitis, Iranians, Iraqis, Libyans, and other members and non-members of OPEC, friends and foes alike.
- The production of global warming gases and urban air pollutants is increased.
- The marginal cost of producing the soft utility portion of these vehicles incurs a non-productive diversion of capital, hardly a prescription for building productive capability.

In other words, if our society devotes money and resources to the futile pursuit of status and/or elegance, we lose some portion of our ability to compete in today's competitive world.

Although no one knows exactly how much capital and resources are devoted to the production and the operation of the soft utility of these vehicles, we cam assume this is no trivial amount. It is possible that, after mature consideration, we will decide that the quest for status and elegance, real or phoney, is an acceptable practice for our more privileged citizens. That debate should consider the inherent inequities and economic inefficiencies imposed upon our society and upon our species.

The quest for status is doomed to eventual, costly failure. The satisfaction one obtains from owning the first Mercedes on the block disappears when the neighbors purchase an equal or more costly status symbol. The Romans and the Renaissance aristocracy recognized the unfortunate consequences of conspicuous consumption; both used "sumptuary" laws to control conspicuous display and its waste. The Romans curbed expenditures on bacchanalia in order to conserve capital and to reduce immoral behavior. The wearing of certain fabrics and garments by the growing merchant class was restricted by Renaissance monarchies and aristocracies. The emerging bourgeois offended by imitating the dress, the habits and the appearance of their "betters."

Would the introduction of rational market forces in the automobile sector correct tendencies toward conspicuous display? We do not know. Our guess is that market incentives will have a healthy effect. We believe, however, that they will not eliminate the problem because this "irrational" behavior is rooted in human nature.

The Feckless Lad

The Los Angeles Times article on the front page of the Metro section featured the photograph of an 18-year-old boy standing next to a van, a popular vehicle a decade or so ago. It reported a "rally" to display "detailing," decorating these vans with ambitious projects of kitsch.

The youth had spent $18,000—his mother's life savings, his entire inheritance—on the detailing of his van. He had eschewed the opportunity to educate himself ($18,000 in those days would have been sufficient for four years at a good university) or to supplement his future income by investing (lending capital) to a productive industry.

The choice he made was neither criminal nor immoral; it was, however, disastrous. Not only for himself, but for society—both should have profited from his mother's foresight and sacrifice in generating savings and capital. Both he and society would have been better off if he had chosen either of the two other options. The Parable of the Feckless Lad and His Van is a metaphor for a portion of middle-class American society. It illustrates the cost of bourgeois efforts to achieve elegance. A society which wastes its money and its resources must reckon with its own impoverishment.

6

SAFETY AND COMMONSENSE

"60 x 10^6 deaths are acceptable in a nuclear war. A society that can stomach 50,000 deaths on the highway each year in peacetime can certainly accept 60 million deaths in wartime."

—Attributed to Herman Kahn

During the 40 days of the Gulf War that were actually violent, Americans lost 146 men and women on the battlefield. During the same 40 days, Americans lost 4,900 men and women to violence—not on the battlefield but on their own highways, in their own country.

We are not suggesting that the Gulf battlefield was safer than American highways; there were somewhat fewer Americans in harm's way in the Gulf War theater. However, if we consider that the exposure to traffic on the home front lasted, for most Americans, only two hours each day, we conclude that Americans in the Gulf were only 30% more at risk than those who spent those same days on the highways "safe" at home.

Streets and roads are public ways that should be safe for everyone. Of course, that's far from the case. Safety comes in graded steps. When among bicyclists, pedestrians are at greater risk than the bicyclists; while on the road, bicyclists are at greater risk than motorists; and motorists are at greater risk than truck drivers. Pedestrians are at the greatest risk of all.

Direct threat to life and limb is not the only concern, since survival in a hazardous environment creates stress and a certain loss of freedom. The choice of making a trip on foot or by bicycle is weighted by the risk from automobiles; we make the trip by auto to reduce our personal risk. By doing so, we increase the risk to others.

Fearing for children walking to school, their parents often drive them. Children are restricted to their yards and sidewalks and denied the freedom to visit friends across the street. Traffic hazards are a serious affliction even to those whose lives and limbs are spared. Although also at risk, the motorist is both the originator of the risk and, yet, is comparatively safe when compared to the pedestrian.

The automobile is dangerous for inherent reasons. It operates in a crowded and competitive environment where skill, acuity, and conscience are needed to maneuver safely. The automobile/freeway system requires large numbers of vehicles to move numbers of people. The potential for collision between vehicles increases exponentially with the number of vehicles. Collisions increase at a more rapid rate than the rate of increase in the number of vehicles.

The mechanical condition of the vehicle is left to the driver whose knowledge, wealth and level of concern must be sufficient to maintain the vehicle in a safe condition. Regular preventive maintenance cannot be ignored until the reminder of a breakdown; brake failures can be disastrous. Overhauls, brake checks, oil changes, lubrication antifreeze and brake fluid additions—are not tasks which arouse enthusiasm. Public transport relieves the traveller of this responsibility. Automobile maintenance, on the other hand, must remain on the minds and consciences of the millions of individuals who own and operate them.

The respective responsibilities of motorist and train operator (particularly when the train is operating along a reserved right-of-way) are illuminating. Maneuvering an automobile is challenging and distracting. The probability of accidents is increased by alcohol, illicit drugs, tobacco and certain prescription drugs; ice or gravel on the roadway adds to the hazard.

The train is guided by tracks and flanged wheels along a line clear of obstructions with signal systems to warn of obstacles. The train comes to a halt when a signal is overlooked. "Dead-man's control" stops the train if the driver is incapacitated. Trains are fitted with interlocks for doors which cannot be opened unless the brakes have been applied.

As the community becomes ever more automobile-dependent, all citizens, even those who are inept, are forced to drive because an adequate alternative is no longer available. In spite of the risk, the driving privilege must not be denied to anyone. The drunks, the recreational drug users and the mentally incompetent must also drive—for the same reason. Our dependence on automotive vehicles having destroyed alternative transportation choices, therefore, has made a productive life without an automobile decidedly unpleasant, if not impossible.

The automobile uses the public ways; in theory, everyone has an equal right to travel. The automobile endangers others such as pedestrians, as well as drivers and passengers. Despite the greater risk to the pedestrian, both driver and pedestrian are regarded as equally responsible under the law.

Where an accident results in death or injury to a pedestrian, the driver may be absolved if there has been no negligence on his part. In choosing the automobile, the driver should assume full moral and financial responsibility. The pedestrian and bicyclist must not be punished with death or dismemberment because of their choice of walking or bicycling.

In deciding to drive, the motorist should be made to accept the responsibility of imposing risks on others. The additional hazard imposed on pedestrians, bicyclists, passengers and other motorists is the direct result of this decision. Furthermore, it is commonplace to encounter drivers who act aggressively, thereby increasing accident probability.

Even if we drive defensively, we are hard-pressed to protect ourselves. Driving requires interaction with many others, among whom are percentages of rage-filled, immature or deranged individuals. Like the handgun, the automobile puts far too much power in the hands of the few who might abuse it.

The operation of large numbers of vehicles, many of whose drivers possess questionable levels of skill and responsibility, is inherently hazardous. National casualties—45,000 deaths and half a million permanent injuries each year—are too high a price to pay for anything, including mobility. The number of automobile deaths we suffer each year are equal to those suffered by the nation in the entire eleven years of the Vietnam war. Automobiles have already killed far more people in the United States than in all of the wars in which the nation has been involved since 1776.

The automobile is the greatest single cause of death among young people. The 16 to 24 year-old age cohort is the only American population group whose life-expectancy is less than it was in 1904 because traffic deaths and gun-shot wounds hit that age-group with the greatest intensity. Adolescent, young males are risk-takers, as attested to by the insurance premiums charged to these drivers. Although auto insurance actuaries may appear to be arbitrary and inequitable when it comes to "redlining" and other practices, they have excellent data and adequate reason with regard to age-related risks.

Freedom of the streets depends on the mode of travel. Walkers and bicyclers can use the streets only with great care but drivers are allowed the greatest possible freedom.

Pedestrians are supposedly protected by laws providing safe crosswalks. Because these laws are difficult to enforce, crosswalks are often removed in the name of safety. It is argued that crosswalks give pedestrians a false sense of security by encouraging them to exercise their right to cross the street. This is the equivalent of placing citizens in prison to protect them from a possible mugging.

Elevated stress levels associated with driving degrades our health and the quality of our lives. Coupled with a sedentary life-style these stress patterns result in increased incidence of stroke and heart attack.

Anonymity and the ability to immediately leave the scene recommends the automobile as a criminal's companion. Statistics (Germany, 1960s) show a correlation between auto ownership and crime. In this country, the neighborhoods immediately surrounding on-ramps to urban freeways are known to be attractive to burglars.

Those who can, remove their families from the presence of the automobile. Homes located on cul-de-sacs are regarded as more desirable. Gated villages and other forms of car-free communities which exclude traffic have become more common. These clustered villages can be designed with amenities, stores, schools and medical offices within walking distance of homes. Dependable transportation connects the community with the nearby metropolis. Where there is less reason to own and maintain an automobile, the citizen lives better and safer; everyone is better off.

If one of the goals of civilization is the increased bodily and spiritual security of the individual, the automotive vehicle is the enemy of civilization and of progress.

7

LAND USE: Developers, Politicians and Highway Engineers— A Symbiotic Relationship

"Time has shown that their vision was inadequate. They have put us into a horrible kind of box committing us to a transportation system that was fundamentally evil."
—Larry Moss, Sierra Club, 1973
[commenting on the original freeway planners]

"Any city planner who thinks that easing the traffic flow will decrease the city's congestion is simply living in a dream world. Likewise the addition of parking facilities will not, and never has, eliminated parking problems. When you improve a small congested road, you wind up with a big congested road. Likewise, the better the traffic pattern, the more traffic on that pattern; the more parking lots, the more people looking for a place to park." —John Keats, *Insolent Chariots*

In the United States, the phrase "urban planning" is an indefensible euphemism. Despite the existence of a large profession which bears this name, urban planners do not plan. They follow along behind the parade of those who do—the land developers. The role of professional planners is to sweep up and organize the dung.

The sprawl of American cities is due to historic forces:

- The symbiotic relationship between developers, political leaders and highway engineers.
- Universal ownership of personal automobiles among the home-buying middle class.
- Cheap mobility for motorists—an artificial market permitting the use of personal automobiles at price levels far below actual cost levels.
- Social problems, particularly the deterioration of central cities.
- Lower taxes and better services enjoyed in the suburbs.
- The tradition of unlimited property rights, permitting the owner to use his land for any purpose, almost without hindrance.

Critics will say this interpretation relies unrealistically on conspiracy theory. We would describe it, instead, as a fortuitous coincidence of interests.

The Politicians

Our democracy has an appalling flaw: the infamous method of financing political campaigns. Local politicians are beholden to developers. We should not be surprised that politicians are compelled to please those who provide campaign funds; the developer, who knows where the buck stops, has long been a cash cow for local political aspirants. They do not discriminate; their gifts go to both parties, with more going to the favored incumbent and to those political candidates who willingly do their bidding.

Campaign funding is a fact of life. Both challengers and incumbents spend the greater part of their time and energy in soliciting funds. Once elected, the office holder must continue the effort; now the purpose is to stay in office and provide huge budgets for campaign staff, postage, printing, rent and media advertising.

Politicians pretend that campaign donors are ideologically motivated; that this is a partisan exercise. The ten-dollar donors may fit that description; the $5,000 and $100,000 donors want something for their money. The argument that donors merely "gain access" is a myth; the reality is that campaign funding is thinly disguised bribery. The fault is ours; the real villain is apathy. We can change the odious business if we wish. Vilifying politicians soothes our souls; it changes nothing.

The Developers

What developers want, they get. This is, of course, maximized profits. They know profits will be maximized by developing land on the periphery of urban areas where the land is cheapest. The two things that they must have are appropriate zoning and highway access obtained through political "friends" in local government .

Political leaders have the authority to change the zoning for land within the boundaries of their jurisdictions. They also have the power to provide or to withhold critical highway access to these lands. Politicians, through their state, city and county engineers, control the location and construction of highways.

The value of land, increased by the ministrations of local authorities urged on by developers, is highly leveraged by this process. The cost of land, of course, is an important component of the cost of housing and commerical projects to the developer. The price of a house, on the other hand, wherever its location, depends on the income of the purchaser, the most important determinant of price. Thus, by placing houses on cheap land on the periphery, developers maximize profits.

It is thought that people choose to buy houses on the periphery of urban areas because these houses offer the most for the money. The facts must be redefined:

- The reason houses are located on the periphery is because that is the furthest location from which homebuyers will drive to their jobs.
- Developers make the decision; that is where they purchase land to make the greatest profit because that is where the cheapest land is located.
- If the young middle-class families who purchase these houses were unwilling or unable to drive so far, the house, with equivalent amenities at the same prices, would then be built at distances from urban centers tolerated by these families.

The $150,000 house for sale in Palmdale (on the periphery of the Los Angeles conurbation) would be the equivalent of a $150,000 house in Pasadena or in Montebello (closer to jobs) if those cities were at the furthest distances that homebuyers were willing to travel. Real estate values, of course, would drop to accommodate the new gradient of geographic convenience. Developers would get rich at a somewhat slower pace.

Homebuying families have criteria; they want a comfortable home within an hour's automobile commute from their jobs, at a price they can afford to pay. They would prefer it to be closer; driving is no longer a pleasant, relaxing recreation for the middle class. Those who shop these subdivisions for homes must have automobiles, probably two per household, if not three or four, depending on the age of the children.

The homebuyer's perception of the cost of driving is critical to this syndrome. The lower the marginal cost of driving, the greater the commute distance that will be tolerated. Free or low-cost parking at work is important to this perception. It not only permits, but seems to mandate, single-occupant automobile-commuting; the automobile has become a necessity; it is no longer a luxury.

Another influence, of course, is middle-class revulsion at the presence of the urban poor, particularly those who combine poverty with a different color or culture. The poor and minorities are left behind in the central cities, bereft of transportation and, hence, of work, recreation, education and other urban amenities. Predictably, their response is to resort to other means of survival. Since middle-class families do not see petty crime and drugs as attractive attributes, their flight is accelerated. Thus, suburbanization—the Los Angelization of our cities.

The Highway Engineer

We do not accuse highway engineers of investing in such obvious conflicts of interest as transit concrete or construction firms. Instead, their conflict is even more compelling. The highway engineer is the fox guarding the chickens. Under the guidance of developers and local government, engineers make the decisions as to where and whether more highways are to be built. They are hardly reluctant, since their careers depend on a continuous stream of highway construction projects. State highway departments employ tens of thousands of people. If their construction programs were to be cut back, they would preside over empty offices. But highway offices are not empty—which testifies to highway engineers' positive view of highways; they have never seen a highway construction project they disliked. Thus, the only limitation on the building of highways is the supply of money. Our political leaders are only too willing to provide that resource through the public purse.

Highway engineers should not have an active role in deciding *if* a highway project should be built. We should recognize that such decisions seriously impact the public interest for better or, usually, for worse. These are political, not technical, decisions. When the decision on a project has been made by others, the engineer's role should become active, not before. They are, or should become, public servants, not decision-makers in the affairs of the public. Highway engineers and civil engineers contribute enormously to this sorcerer's apprentice syndrome. The tendency of developers to buy cheap, peripheral land for their projects depends on confidence that compliant local public works departments and/or state highway agencies can be persuaded to build highways, usually at public expense, to furnish automotive access even before bulldozers move onto housing sites. This is a significant part of the circular process which has led the nation into automotive dependency.

When new houses are built on the periphery of urban areas, demand for transportation is increased. Thus, building a highway generates demand for more travel; given current American conditions, it cannot possibly satisfy it.

Conclusion

The word "city" cannot be applied to the American form of urban life; only the centers of the American conurbations fit the meaning of the word. American cities may become real cities in the long-term, but only after corrupting influences—campaign funding, automotive subsidies and political and career-tainted decisions regarding highway projects—have been rectified. Only then will professional planners be free to plan cities meant to serve the human race. Only then will we be freed of our environmental, economic and social ills.

8

ECONOMICS

"The natural effort of every individual to better [their] own condition, when suffered to exert itself with freedom and security, is so powerful a principle, that it is alone and without assistance . . . capable of surmounting a hundred impertinent obstructions with which the folly of human laws too often incumbers its operation."

—Adam Smith, *The Wealth of Nations*

It is said that Reagan White House staffers were fond of Adam Smith neckties. And that the halls of government rang with quotes from the books of Milton Friedman. Adam Smith's "invisible hand" is the substance of the American ideology. Despite this lip service, however, the nation has strayed far from the paths recommended by Adam Smith. The transition back to a free market is the terrible problem facing the Soviet Union, China and Eastern Bloc nations; it also confronts the United States.

How Capitalist is the United States?

Fascinated, we watch the Eastern Bloc nations struggling to return to the market system. Americans preen themselves in the belief that they are apostles of that system and are proud that they were right all along. Americans think themselves immune from the remarkable inefficiencies of the Leninist/Stalinist economic syndrome; this is an absurdity.

With regard to the costs associated with the operation of automobiles and trucks, their infrastructure and associated services, perhaps the largest portion of the American economy, economic practice is more akin to Lenin and Stalin than to Adam Smith; Milton Friedman is honored more in the breach. And, predictably, economic abuse and wild extravagance are the rule.

The Soviet Problem

The free market is essential to any society, but particularly to a free society. It is the economic equivalent of political democracy since it gives consumers power regarding the characteristics of the products offered by producers; it gives them the power to choose which goods and which manufacturer, how much, what sizes, which colors and how many models shall be provided. The providers have incentives to woo more of the consumers' dollar-votes by offering the best they can at the lowest prices.

Consumers are treated with deference in the free market; they are given the ultimate choice. Producers have powerful incentives to adopt efficient methods, manage their labor, material sources and transport efficiently and effectively to provide the best quality for the least price. No other system can achieve this result.

Consider two competing brands of bread on a market shelf: if the total cost of baking each of the loaves, wrapping them and getting them to the store shelf is fully reflected in the price (unlike the price of Gorbachev's "rolls"), consumers will be able to choose wisely; selections will be based on honest comparisons of value. Honest prices will transmit knowledge of the real costs. Producers, in turn, will have every reason to carefully watch all aspects of production to the end that quality will be maximized, costs and prices minimized. The market mechanism ensures that the most attractive product is made available to consumers at fair prices.

Now let us consider a case in which prices are corrupted. Suppose a portion of the cost is borne by a subsidy—one producer is favored by the mayor of the city who furnishes *this* baker with free rent; while the competitor is not so lucky. Now the price of the loaf produced by the first baker no longer represents its real cost. The bread has not actually become cheaper. In fact, its real cost will be *greater* than the cost of the competitor's loaves because the mayor's friend will have been relieved of a portion of the constraints which normal, honest competition provides; the mayor's friend's costs will rise. But the consumers will not be informed. The effect of the subsidy is plainly egregious:

- The purchaser can no longer make rational comparisons between competing products because the price of one is rigged.
- The mayor's baker friend is no longer compelled to provide the best quality at the lowest price.
- The unsubsidized baker faces an unfair market, thereby losing market share.
- The taxpayer sees taxes rise since the subsidies enjoyed by the mayor's friend are provided from public funds.

An observer, noting how well the subsidized bread sells, might conclude that consumers actually prefer that product to the other. Those who have a vested interest in marketing the subsidized bread might intimidate those who would reduce the largesse enjoyed by the mayor's friend. The result is analogous to corrupt politicians who hide their real character, distort their views and positions on issues. Voters, like consumers buying the subsidized bread, cast their votes based on incorrect facts. The public interest suffers.

Policies pertaining to the car/truck/highway sector bear a family resemblance to those designed by Stalin for the economic architecture of the Soviet Union. In his attempt to achieve the objectives of Marxism-Leninism, Stalin eliminated the market-mechanism in a blind, catastrophic leap of faith. One Soviet agency, Gosplan, in

Moscow, set prices, arbitrarily, for the millions of articles sold in the vast nation. Gosplan also provided capital, managed, and set standards and production quotas for Soviet factories, mines and agriculture. The consequences for the Soviet economy and for the Soviet people have been predictable and devastating.

The Gosplan process was the economics of the insane asylum. It has had enormously damaging results for Soviet citizens—wasteful use of resources, shortages of consumer and other goods and services, environmental abuse and low motivational levels in all worker and manager echelons—plus the effects of a massive, infinitely powerful bureaucracy run amok.

The significance of the free market as the indispensable planning mechanism for a nation-sized economy is revealed by the absurdity of the Stalinist experiment. Russia's road to sanity is reliance on market mechanisms.

The planning done by American state highway departments and by the federal Department of Transportation (DOT) has much in common with Gosplan planning. Decisions as to whether and where a highway is to be built depend heavily on political and bureaucratic maneuvering, on pork barrel and on subsidies. The level of ownership and the use of automotive vehicles depend on massive subsidies (on the vast differences between the real cost and the price the user pays). The effects on the Soviet economy were worse because the principles we apply to our car/truck/highway sector (25% of our economy) were applied to the entire Soviet economy.

Market Forces in the Transportation Sector

The business of manufacturing and selling vehicles is governed by the market. The manufacturer attempts to maximize profits; prices are set to cover costs. The dealer, pressed by both the manufacturer and the buyer, reacts to honest market forces but again prices must also reflect costs. The mechanic and the body and fender man do what they do for the same reasons. The purchaser, although often motivated by vanity, not by utility, does respond to price. Prices reflect actual costs. Common sense, acquisitive instincts (greed), and the marketplace function as they should.

The vehicles are the easy part.

Our concern is not with vehicles, but with the costs of vehicle parking and operation, with the costs of local government services, and with the costs of the construction and maintenance of highways. In these areas, the prices the driver pays do *not* reflect real costs. The market for space and services, given these conditions, cannot function properly. In fact, it has never functioned as it should.

For those who believe that we have no economic problems, it will be useful to examine some of our critical indicators:

- Real wages in the United States have not risen since 1970.
- The economy has not prospered and both public and private debt has risen sharply.

- The federal debt has tripled.
- Banks and, particularly, the savings and loan industry have had to be rescued from scandalous decrepitude.

Deficit borrowings by the federal government and the losses which propelled the S & L industry towards disaster pumped hundreds of billions into the economy. Are these financial anomalies part of the reason for the curious prosperity of the recent past?

The nation has regressed, not in absolute terms, but in comparison with other industrial powers. The huge aggregate cost of the automobile/truck/highway sector has drained off household surpluses. These should have entered investment channels by way of personal savings accounts and bond and equity markets. The automobile/truck/highway/services sector demands in great quantities two of the four important elements essential to industrial productivity, land and capital—the other two are labor and raw materials.

At this writing we are in what appears to be a "recession." This iteration of a frequent event in our economy now has a scary aspect; no one really knows the effect of the enormous public and private debt. From 1980 to 1990, corporate debt increased 60% in constant dollars; household debt increased in the same proportion. External debt increased five-fold to over $500 billion. The interest payments on this debt constitute an enormous burden on the nation's producers. Those who produce pay those who hold bonds; not a desirable condition for a nation whose competitiveness is in serious question.

We consume more, save less, and invest less. We, therefore, produce less. We are no longer the wealthiest nation. Our productivity growth rate is less than that of many of the world's industrial nations. We see Japan and Germany overtaking and surpassing us; other nations, notably Sweden and Switzerland, have done so long ago.

There is an inclination to think that the successes of Japan and Germany are due to cheating in international trade—violating GATT rules.

GATT (the General Agreement on Tariffs and Trade) is a continuing negotiation among the industrialized nations to reduce trade barriers. Tariffs are only the most obvious of such barriers; unreasonable quality requirements, unofficial agreements in industry to "buy Japanese" (for instance) and agricultural and other subsidies may be even more important.

Such cheating as does exist does not explain the huge Japanese and German trade surpluses. The reality is that the practices of Japan, Germany or the others are not significantly at fault; they act in their own best interest. Their success is due, primarily, to greater efficiency and industrial productivity. We are not as productive as our competitors.

How has this come about?

The automobile began life in Europe as a plaything for the aristocracy and the wealthy where the spirit of the time was, in part, old-fashioned Fabian socialism; a "soak the rich" philosophy established, fortuitously, a rational level of taxation for vehicle use.

In the United States, a contrary view of the automobile was held. The automobile was regarded as a device to rescue farmers from mud and isolation and the middle-class from boredom. The Model T was God-given; Henry Ford was God. Getting the nation "out of the mud" was the slogan of the automobile industry and the highway builders of that time.

The community absorbed virtually all the cost. When the first few autos in town created a need for a traffic policeman, he was paid from the general fund, not from an assessment on the drivers who incurred the need for his services.

The early automobile clubs, the highway builders, the truckers and the manufacturers began what was to become a remarkably effective special-interest institution—the highway lobby. It became the voice of the automotive interests.

Its vigorous campaign frustrates efforts to shift costs to the motorists and the trucking industry—the users—who receive the benefits and who should pay the cost of highways and services. The highway lobby still defends these policies.

In its early years, the highway lobby was firmly opposed to the imposition of *any* taxes to fund the construction and maintenance of highways or other services to the motorist or trucker fearing that such taxes would discourage automobile ownership and reduce demand for the products of the struggling industry.

Only later did they recognize that a program of improving existing roads and constructing new roads was essential to the expansion of their markets. With some reluctance, the highway lobby permitted taxes to be levied on motorists and on the trucking industry since it was more difficult to get highways built with funds from other sources.

Sequestration

While accepting that minimal taxes should be imposed, the lobby insisted the yield should be sequestered for the sole purposes of road construction and maintenance. Fighting under these two flags of determined illogic, they have been remarkably successful. The Great American highway does, indeed, belong in part to Buick (which now must share it with Toyota and BMW). Fuel taxes have been held to absurdly inadequate levels; highways and parking lots have proliferated like daffodills in spring-time.

Virtually all states, as well as the federal government, have constitutional provisions which prevent the use of fuel tax and other excise tax funds for other purposes, even for many automobile-associated expenses. The lobby has been abetted in this by politicians, developers, automobile clubs, state highway departments, highway contractors, construction labor and, of course, highway engineers.

The sequestering of fuel tax funds is one of the curiosities of American local and state government; the yields of no other tax have been dedicated to the needs of a special interest group. Furthermore, sequestration does not require that expenditures for highway needs be limited to the sequestered funds, the yield of the fuel tax or of any other tax.

Since the fuel tax and other user fees do not generate sufficient funds to satisfy the needs of highways and services, and since highway infrastructures have priority, the other services provided by local government—schools, libraries, police and fire protection—are underfunded; schools deteriorate, police departments are understaffed. Never mind; potholes get fixed, traffic signals installed, parking structures built. Property tax yields are routinely raided to pay the bills incurred by the motorist. When motorists leave their cars, however, they leave their privileges behind. When their homes are burglarized, they discover the police department can only sympathize. If they complain about the quality of schools, they discover school district budgets are inadequate and teachers demoralized. None of this prevents taxpayers from complaining about the shortcomings of public services. Unfortunately, their most vigorous complaints are reserved for potholed or unswept streets.

Society should take a page out of the highway lobby's book; property and sales tax revenues should be sequestered, as well, to prevent their diversion to the needs of motorists and the trucking industry. Property and/or sales tax levels should be reduced or eliminated—gas tax levels would, of necessity, rise to fill the need.

Dependence on automotive vehicles imposes heavy costs on American communities. Despite this the network of infrastructure, roads, arterials, freeways, bridges, drains, traffic signals, parking lots—hundreds of billions of dollars invested over the ninety-odd years of the automobile age—are offered free for the sole use of motorists and truckers.

The exemption of road transport from full-cost pricing creates a massive inequity in competition between railways and trolley lines on the one hand and road users on the other. The railroads and urban transit firms built their own facilities and paid appropriate property and other taxes. Road users did neither. Automobiles, trucks and highways multiplied; free-enterprise transit systems and railroads degenerated.

In the late 19th century, the public image of the railroads and transit firms was sullied by the raunchy reputation of the robber barons and the monopolies they generated and exploited. This reputation still poisons the debate.

The railroads and transit firms, perhaps recognizing their vulnerability due to the persistence and prevalence of this myth, have been curiously inactive, even reticent, in protecting political and economic turf and have suffered as a result. It is said that the American railroads are daunted by the trucking industry. It is true that the American Trucking Association has a highly effective and aggressive lobby in the halls of Washington and state capitols.

The corruption of the market forces which operate in the highway sector has produced important detrimental effects. The money used to pay costs incurred by the motorist is derived from increased property and sales taxes, increased retail prices and and decreased paychecks.

Conclusion

In other words, we are using our own money to bribe ourselves to use—to excess—our automobiles and trucks. As a result, we have generated serious economic, societal and environmental problems. These same policies have destroyed our public transit lines, necessitating even more subsidies from the public purse. For truly world-class absurdity, the only possible comparison is with Gosplan.

9

ENVIRONMENTAL, POLITICAL AND SOCIAL EFFECTS

"When kids get wheels, parents lose constructive control of their behavior."   —Anonymous

As a contributor to the destruction of the environment, the automobile has few peers. It is far more than a mere air polluter. Its exhaust is only the most visible of its impacts; it generates greenhouse gases, acid rain and ozone depletors. American automobiles and trucks contribute about one billion tons of CO_2 per year to the atmosphere, plus tremendous volumes of nitrous oxides and CFCs—all global warming gases.

American cars and trucks consume 20% of the oil produced on the planet. Traffic deaths and injuries, urban sprawl, the enormous appetite for space, the resulting pressure on urban real estate—all these are products of American dependence on automotive vehicles.

Each automobile tire loses about one pound of rubber per year; four pounds of rubber dust are generated by each vehicle. The loss from heavy truck and bus tires is greater. No definitive study has been made regarding the effects of this dust. However, we assume that the smaller dust particles are sent off into the surrounding air, to remain suspended (and inhaled) for substantial periods of time. Larger particles drop more quickly to the ground; all particles either bind on the road surface or migrate to neighboring unpaved areas where they remain in the soil indefinitely or until they are oxidized.

Since metal-to-metal contact in brakes and clutches cannot be tolerated, heat-resistant pads consisting of fabric and a binder are placed between brake and clutch elements. Until recently, the only usable fabric was asbestos, a carcinogen now being removed from schools and offices.

Its use in clutches and brakes continued long after it was banned from buildings. As a component of automobiles, asbestos is a greater hazard than when enclosed passively within the walls of a building; the fibers are ground off and dispersed widely as dust. It has recently been replaced but the substitute materials are still converted to dust. It is hoped that the new materials will prove less dangerous.

Concrete and asphalt paving create other problems. Rain water normally adds itself to ground water by percolation through the soil. Paving prevents this; ground water is not replenished; run-off is increased, causing erosion and flooding. Enhanced runoff volumes are normally channeled in concrete until they reach a river or the sea.

The automobile consists of two tons of metal, glass, rubber and plastic. Its lifespan is seven to ten years; 17 million or more are discarded each year in the nation. While most are recycled or cannibalized in scrap yards at the end of their lives, others are left to rust away at curbsides, driveways and front yards. During the 1960s, New York City reported that more than 200 discarded automobiles were abandoned each day. The amount of recoverable material is small; the conversion of recycled materials and parts is accomplished only with the expenditure of energy, transportation and materials.

Automotive vehicles are noisy. The sound of internal combustion engines and of tires rubbing on the pavement, plus vehicles with inadequate mufflers, loud horns, alarms and sound systems, all add to the unfortunate effect.

Off-road vehicles affect even the wilderness. There is no place to hide from the automobile; no way to avoid its impact on our lives.

Automotive Fuels

The preparation, distribution and storage of automotive fuels also produce egregious effects. Refineries are serious polluters contributing odors, noxious gases and smoke. Oil and gasoline leakage from refinery and storage tanks into the ground water is commonplace.

Gasoline is transported to distribution points by trucks. These emit their own exhaust and tire-rubber pollution. Accidents involving gasoline tank trucks have created catastrophic fires. Underground gasoline storage tanks are a serious source of ground water pollution because of leakage from corroded tanks. It is estimated that between 25,000 to 50,000 gas station storage tanks are leaking into underlying aquifers.

Politics and the Automobile

Misinformation regarding the effects of automobiles plagues our political decisions. The highway lobby belittles these problems, thus encouraging the wide-spread use of automobiles. This is cited, disingenously, as proof of public preference, ignoring the corrupted market forces which are the actual causal factor.

Measures to increase user fees are invariably met with vigorous opposition. All the middle-class—literate, prosperous, productive, working and voting citizens—are motorists. Political leaders prudently avoid the question, being aware that universal automobile ownership and of the persistance and effectiveness of the myth is a formidable barrier to corrective action.

An important factor in the politics of the fuel tax is that the yield from a one cent (one percent) increase in the sales tax is about equal to that from a ten cents per gallon increase in the fuel tax. The fuel tax appears to be the larger, although the yield is the same. Legislators regard the sales tax as being a less hazardous political path. If the choice is between increasing the fuel tax or the sales tax, it appears invariably the sales tax which is chosen to be increased. Furthermore, the yield of the sales tax is not sequestered as is that of the fuel tax.

The American automobile has an important impact on global politics. Domestic oil production is not adequate to meet the national demand for gasoline; we are dependent on imported oil to satisfy our needs.

Often the countries supplying us are unfriendly and unstable. The OPEC and other oil-producing nations control the oil upon which we have made ourselves dependent. These nations and their leaders purchase American industries and real estate with the proceeds. They arm themselves with the latest artillery, missiles and fighter planes. Several of their leaders believe that their thumbs will soon be on the American carotid artery. We have recently fought a war whose origins were derived from this syndrome. The Gulf War began in our prodigal dependence on oil from that region.

Social Impacts of the Automobile

Automobile dependence and its consequence—universal automobile ownership among the middle-class—has converted American cities into sprawled, isolated bedroom communities on the model of Los Angeles. Americans are alienated because of their isolation from one another in their vehicles and in their suburbs; hostile drivers rage at each other, competing for scarce road space; society is falsely stratified because of a phony status conferred by certain vehicles.

The isolation of driver and passengers from pedestrians permits deadly forms of crime: drive-by shootings, hurling rocks from overpasses, deliberate use of the automobile as a weapon. The anonymity of drivers and passengers and their ability to make a fast escape recommend the automobile to petty criminals.

A transportation system that shares scarce space among many participants must, of necessity, be civilized. However, drivers cannot always master their emotions. Hostile gestures following a real or imagined "cut-off" of one vehicle by another are an American tradition, though not unknown elsewhere. In recent years the gesture has been accompanied by gunfire.

Alienation begins with young children isolated in the family automobile who grow up in a world in which they have little real contact with adults outside the family circle. The experience of occasionally riding in common-carrier transportation would provide healthier environment, including contacts with older strangers. An exchange is beneficial for both: the child learns something of the protocols and joys of conversation, the stranger enjoys a few moments with the child.

Land use is distorted by the automobile and its insatiable appetite for space. Planning for housing and commercial uses is determined more by automobile-related considerations than by the needs of people since planners must first provide space for parking and for roads. This requirement is clearly antithetical to human convenience for it generates additional auto use.

The scattering of people in the low density conurbations dictated by automobile dependency places people beyond easy walking distance from friends, shopping, jobs and schools. The cycle is circular. The automobile, because of its space requirements and because it is a significant part of the mechanism impelling urban growth, increases the demand for travel.

The myth: the automobile satisfies travel demand. The reality: far from satisfying demand, it increases demand.

Conclusion

Our nation is dedicated to freedom and to the profound conviction that legitimacy in governance must rest on the consent of the governed. That is a view of government which is not only noble and moral, it is also practical. Price reform and the application of free market principles to automobile, truck and highway use would extend this philosophy to a critical segment of our economy.

Consumers need to recognize the full cost of their consumption; this requires that they pay prices which reflect actual incurred costs for goods and services. The essential element of the marketplace is the linkage by which prices transmit honest and accurate cost information to consumers. If they are deprived of accurate information, consumers will make unwise and distorted choices. Where goods and services are underpriced, market forces inexorably lead to excess consumption.

10

SUSTAINABILITY AND FOREIGN POLICY

"The cost of a gallon of gas in the U.S. has reached its lowest level ever. It does not reflect the cost of defense for the Middle East, smog, global warming or the trade imbalance caused by oil imports. Gasoline prices in Europe and Japan are double or triple the U.S. price because governments there impose levies that force consumers to consider and internalize the full costs of their behavior. If Americans want to hold down oil consumption and attendant carbon dioxide emissions and play a world leadership role, a revision of transportation policy to reflect all energy-related costs would be a good place to start."

—John H. Gibbons, Peter D. Blair and Holly Gwin, "Strategies for Energy Use," *Scientific American*, September 1989

The energy needs of the American automobile/truck/highway system far exceed those of a more rational combination of transportation modes. This should include a network of public transportation and railroads. The consumption of gasoline and diesel fuel in the United

States is four times as great as per capita consumption in Europe.

The automobile/truck/highway sector is our greatest single consumer of energy. Automotive vehicles are also wasteful in the use of energy for moving people and goods; their energy needs must include not only operation but vehicle manufacture and the construction and maintenance of highway infrastructure. The magnitude is barely recognized.

Currently, even if we exclude oil normally pumped in Kuwait and Iraq, oil is in surplus; there may be a 20% excess pumping capacity above present levels of worldwide consumption. There is some disagreement as to when this surplus will be exhausted but eventually oil will become scarce. Worldwide, the annual consumption of oil is 21 billion barrels. Production rates are approximately zero.

The word "production" is misused by the oil industry. The proper term is "extraction;" American automobiles are consuming a finite resource. The oil industry has little desire or reason to prolong the life of the earth's petroleum resources for conservation would not increase the industry's profit levels. On the contrary, as oil becomes scarce, as it must in the next few decades under existing regimes, oil prices will rise steeply and oil industry profits will increase sharply.

The industry wants us to believe that prosperity depends on present levels of consumption. What spells prosperity for the industry is poverty for all the rest of us. We are impoverishing ourselves, our children and our children's children by our profligate use of oil and other nonrenewable energy sources.

Natural gas, coal and oil shale are either potential motor fuels or precursor materials from which motor fuels can be manufactured in commercial quantities. We are told that we have several hundred years supply of these in reserve; not to worry. While there is a partial truth in this, we are not told another truth. As these stocks are drawn upon, these fuels too will become much more expensive.

Wood is another source of energy. The situation of the world's forests, in contrast to that of other fuel sources, has touched our imaginations. Vast areas of the earth's surface have been denuded of forests because of the need to satisfy the requirements of inhabitants for farm and pasture land, for lumber and firewood. In England, Greece, Italy and in portions of the great plains of North America, this process of deforestation was completed hundreds of years ago.

The deforestation process is continuing at accelerated rates in the Amazon Basin, in India, Nepal, Thailand, Malaysia, Madagascar and Burma. As the prices of oil and of other hydrocarbon fuels rise because of increasing scarcity, the poor of the third world will be forced to turn more and more to the forests for fuel. Thus, feedback from excessive oil consumption can only accelerate the destruction of the world's forests.

The burning of the Amazon rain forests has been fostered by policies as ill-conceived as those of our own society and government as well as by the great need of

Brazilians for farm and grazing land. The driving engine of this process in Brazil as well as in other nations, such as Madagascar and Burma, is the third world poverty of people who are not only poor, but have little opportunity for productive employment.

Forestry practices, in advanced nations such as the United States and Sweden, are designed to produce sustained yields of timber, but offer little grounds for optimism regarding the success of this effort or of the future of the forests. These projects frequently result in single-species forests with trees planted in serried ranks bearing little resemblance to the original forest and, hence, offering only poor habitat for the animal species displaced in the destruction of the original forest.

The Greenhouse Effect

The destruction of the world's forests has focused on its effects on the earth's climate. The Greenhouse Effect is as yet unproven, but suspiciously credible. The effect of the putative climatic change is still unknown and may not be felt for years. However, the hypotheses, which are now common currency among serious scientists, are frightening. Important portions of the planet's cropland could be rendered unusable; fertile areas might have to be relocated and major changes affecting the amount of such land might be the result (we cannot know whether food production will be reduced or enhanced). It is believed, in the more dramatic scenarios, that the level of the sea might rise, wiping out many of the harbors of the world and otherwise reshaping the shorelines of the world's oceans.

The forests, the oceans and the earth's rocks are "sinks" or reservoirs for quantities of the planet's carbon. Carbon is retained in trees and other vegetation in the form of wood fiber and other carbohydrates; it is retained in the oceans and in limestone and marble in the form of calcium carbonate.

The earth's atmosphere is laced with CO_2, a molecule which absorbs the infrared reflection from the earth's surface. The CO_2 in the atmosphere in prehistoric times has been found to be about 280 parts per million (from analysis of ancient air embedded in the earth's great ice fields and glaciers). The atmosphere's burden of CO_2 has been directly monitored for three decades; its proportion is increasing. It has now reached 340 parts per million (20% over prehistoric levels). The cause of the increase is, without doubt, the burning of the planet's fossil fuels, which are also reservoirs for ancient carbon—carbon is once more released as CO_2 into the atmosphere.

It is estimated that CO_2 accounts for somewhat more than half the warming, whereas CFCs and methane account for about equal parts of the remainder.

The total respiration (cycling) of carbon is about 100 billion tons per year: 5.6 billion tons come from the burning of fossil fuels, 3 billion tons from deforestation. The remainder the normal production of carbon dioxide from the oxidation of vegetation and exhalations of animal life. The annual increase of carbon dioxide in the earth's atmosphere appears to be about 4 billion tons per year; the increase has accumulated in a very brief period.

The greenhouse warming phenomenon may also be accompanied by a feedback mechanism (a snowballing effect). Rates of respiration (metabolic burning of carbon with release of energy, carbon dioxide and water) increase with temperature; an increase of 10°C may increase carbon dioxide production by a factor of two or three. A 1°C increase may increase it by 10, 20 or 30%. This implies that an open-ended warming process may have catastrophic, irreversible, results.

To stabilize the atmosphere at this level, it appears necessary to reduce the current level of release of CO_2 by least four billion tons annually. The 5.6 billion tons released from fossil fuels and the one to three billion tons from deforestation are the only two sources that can be physically controlled. A four-billion-ton annual reduction cannot be achieved without a minimum 60% reduction in the use of fossil fuels together with a cessation of deforestation.[*] However, any significant effort at controlling either fossil fuel consumption or deforestation must be preceded by agreements of unprecedented difficulty.

CO_2 is not the only greenhouse gas; nitrogen oxides, CFCs and methane in the earth's atmosphere also trap heat. Nitrogen constitutes four-fifths of the air we breathe; the burning of fossil fuels generates CO_2; in addition, the nitrogen present is converted to nitrogen

---

[*] From an interview with George M. Woodwell, Director, Wood's Hole Research Center, reported in *Calypso*, June 1991.

oxide. The CFCs are the refrigeration gases now used in air conditioners and refrigerators and are also active in depleting atmospheric ozone.

The Carbon Tax

The price we pay for consuming fossil fuels should include the cost of preserving the planet's atmosphere and its climate. The carbon tax, a fee paid by individual consumers to compensate for their use of fossil fuels, is a concept that would rationalize aberrant economic incentives; it would inhibit consumption.

The carbon tax yield should also be used to finance programs to halt deforestation, replant the planet's forests, maintain them and to take such other measures as are necessary to achieve these goals. The yield could be used to pay the governments of countries such as Brazil, Malaysia and Burma to maintain their forests. These nations would hire their own people to plant trees, to maintain and expand the remaining forests and to defend them against destruction.

Both the government and the population would have substantive incentives to act responsibly. Local labor could be paid with local, soft currencies. The government would use the hard currencies thus earned to repay existing debts and to invest in their infrastructure, their educational system and in productive industries. With restored credit and a productive labor force, third world nations would have a real opportunity to make the difficult transition to viable, stable societies and economies. The forests would be given an economic value appropriate to their real value. The planet and its ecosystems might be given a chance.

The carbon tax should be designed to generate enough yield to finance the reforestation effort at appropriate levels; it should also be sufficient to ensure a more intelligent, inhibited consumption level of the world's remaining reservoir of fossil fuels.

The Hubbert Curve

The life of the earth's petroleum resources and the certainty of future oil scarcities have been addressed by King Hubbert, a petroleum geologist who devised a theory encompassing future oil discoveries, extraction and scarcity which has been accepted by some. Hubbert shows that we passed the peak of oil extraction capacity a decade ago. Since then, confirmed exploitable oil reserves have been shrinking. The Hubbert peak arrived in the mid-1970s only 120 years after the beginning of the oil era. Since worldwide extraction is in surplus over consumption by about 20%, this surplus of oil keeps the price between $15 and $25 per barrel. When the surplus disappears, as it must, the price will rise steeply.

If consumption continues at present levels, the Hubbert Curve shows that supply will meet the consumption curve in about 25 years (but consumption has been increasing in recent years by as much as $1\frac{1}{2}\%$ annually— thus, the Hubbert intersection may occur earlier).

At that point, the surplus extractive capacity will have vanished; humanity will be at the mercy of the oil industry, the members of OPEC and other oil-extracting nations. The history of the oil industry, of our political leaders and of humanity itself does not inspire confidence that we will meet that challenge with intelligence.

It is simplistic to speak of the "end" of oil extraction; it will certainly continue for centuries to come. Oil is highly valuable as a raw material, even at high prices and in small quantities. It is not that oil consumption will end; it is more accurate to describe the phenomenon as an "increasing scarcity" of oil which will bring with it a concurrent and rapid increase in oil prices.

High prices, of course, will reduce consumption but they will also increase inflationary pressures as they did after the oil shocks of 1973 and 1978. The sudden increase in the price of oil will also exacerbate international tensions surrounding the possession of the remaining oil reserves. Increased oil prices will generate interest in other sources of energy, particularly those which can be refined into liquid fuels. Conversion of oil shales, of coal and of methane to gasoline will become front page news once again. Given increased prices, the use of biological sources—sugar cane, corn, vegetative and other waste for raw material will become possible.

Whatever measures we take to deal with the energy problem, it is certain that fuel of all sorts will be more expensive. It is important to our childrens' and their childrens' life-style that we use more intelligence than we have displayed in the past.

The earth's reserves of oil are being rapidly depleted. Future generations will find little oil available even at very high prices. Drilling for oil—whether off-shore or on—may produce some productive fields; it may prolong the agony another few years.

It cannot create more oil.

Energy Efficiency

Automobiles and trucks are energy wasters for a number of reasons:

- **Tires**
  Rubber tires, essential to absorb pavement shock, also consume energy, generating heat because of internal friction due to flexing of tread and sidewalls and the friction generated by contact with the pavement.
- **Wind resistance**
  Automotive vehicles incur much more air resistance than equivalent vehicles formed into a train. The air resistance generated at the sides, tops and ends of the separate vehicles increases the energy required for propulsion.
- **Weight**
  The energy of acceleration increases with the weight of the vehicle. The weight per passenger, assuming 1.1 passengers, of the average two-ton urban automobile is 3,636 lbs. A streetcar weigh-

ing 17 tons and carrying 200 passengers weighs 170 lbs. per passenger.

Of course, 1.1 passengers per automobile is not the largest possible number. However, attempts to persuade commuters to carpool have demonstrated that the urban-commuting or shopping automobile is highly unlikely to increase its average occupant load under any circumstances. Even at the maximum number, six, the vehicle weight per passenger is still 500 lbs., considerably more than the streetcar.

- **Fuel Tanks**
  Automobiles and trucks must carry their energy. This adds considerably to the weight of the vehicle; energy is consumed to transport energy. Electric rail vehicles do not have this disadvantage.
- **Fuel Transportation**
  Gasoline must be supplied to automobiles at locations remote from oil fields and gasoline refineries. Energy is required to move oil or gasoline by truck or pipeline.
- **Fuel Manufacture**
  The refining process in which gasoline and diesel oil are distilled from petroleum requires the expenditure of considerable energy. Over 12% of the oil is consumed in the distillation process.

- **Deceleration Energy**

  In normal operation, automobiles and trucks decelerate as well as accelerate. In decelerating, they use the friction of their brakes to absorb the kinetic energy (momentum) of the vehicle. Since the vehicle has no ability (except for certain electric cars) to conserve this energy, it is lost to the atmosphere in the form of heat. An electric rail system, connected to a central power system, is capable of regenerative braking; braking by absorbing the kinetic energy of the train and conserving it by pouring it back into the power grid.[*]

- **Power Transmission**

  The internal combustion engine has certain inherent inefficiencies and complexities in its power train. Because at low-engine speeds the torque is limited, the engines must run at moderate to high speeds; they rotate in only one direction. Multi-ratio transmissions are used to convert high-engine torque at high engine speeds to low road speeds; transmissions are also necessary to reverse the direction of travel. Transmissions consume energy because of friction in gears, bearings and clutches.

---

[*] This system was used successfully early in the 20th century by the Chicago, Milwaukee, St. Paul and Pacific Railroad.

- **Engine Cooling**
  Internal combustion engines operate at high temperatures. Excess heat is exhausted through the tail pipe and radiator, both major losses and sources of inefficiency.

- **Limited Life**
  The short life—six years on average—incurs a heavy cost in energy needed to salvage the hulks and manufacture new vehicles.

- **Traffic Signals**
  Traffic signals are complex, sophisticated and energy intensive. A busy intersection may have 42 red, green and amber lights, more turn signals, pedestrian "walk" lights and in-pavement sensors. Such intersections often consume more electricity than a large home.

- **Highways**
  Construction of highways requires earth moving, compaction of fills and building of bridges and pavements consuming large amounts of energy. Pavement repairs, sweeping, maintenance of signs and collision barriers continue in perpetuity.

American trucks consume 1.2 billion barrels of fuel/year; railroads about 0.2 billion (1989). Trucks consume 15 times as much fuel per ton/mile as rail freight trains. A 20% shift of freight from trucks to railroads would save the nation about 220 million barrels of oil per year.

Inadequate energy reserves, particularly oil, will be an increasingly serious problem for humanity in the decades ahead. Solutions are essential to the long-term sustainability of existing systems. Present levels of consumption are outrageously excessive.

The consequences, of course, are felt by all inhabitants of the planet, not only by American drivers. The cost of gasoline consumed in a Rolls Royce in Beverly Hills is also paid for by tribal members in the heart of Africa buying kerosene for their cooking fires.

The price we pay for energy does not reflect the essential finiteness of the material, its importance to humanity or the cost of meeting the challenge of global warming. The carbon tax would help to rectify this deviation from free market principles and create a healthier pricing structure and a more vital economy.

11

REGRESSIVITY AND THE FUEL TAX

"Annual income twenty pounds, annual expenditure nineteen pounds nineteen and six, result happiness. Annual income twenty pounds, annual expenditure twenty pounds ought and six, result misery." —Charles Dickens, *David Copperfield*

We are advised by Diana Furchgott-Roth* that increased motor fuel taxes would constitute a large burden on the small income of the poor, a small burden on the large income of the rich. If forced to adopt her carefully focused view, we would have to admit that she is right.

The Furchgott-Roth statement is readily understood; we assume that the average driver uses 500 gallons of gasoline per year and that the state plus federal fuel tax is 28 cents per gallon. Such a driver pays $140 in fuel taxes annually, amounting to 1.4% of the income for a

---

* *The Regressivity of Motor Fuel Excise Taxes*, American Petroleum Institute, March 1988

person earning $10,000; for an income of $200,000 it is less than 0.1% (persons earning less than $10,000 are assumed not to own automobiles). Since it is probable that the wealthy consume more gasoline than the poor, the relationship may be tempered slightly. This seems to corroborate the Furchgott-Roth conclusion. On this basis the tax is regressive.

But only on this basis.

Ms. Furchgott-Roth, because she is either disingenuous or careless, has overlooked several relevant aspects of the question. She has forgotten that the cost of automobiles to owners and to society is far more than the cost of the fuel tax. A careful examination of the problem—the American urban poor, joblessness and the underclass—would show that a higher fuel tax would result in a situation contrary to regressiveness; it would be broadly progressive. It would produce significant direct and indirect benefits to the poor and to the underclass (and to all of us), at a lesser burden to them (and to us), not only in taxes, but in retail prices and in other ways as well. Questions of equity are also relevant.

Property and Sales Taxes

Drivers are spared most of the cost of city and county services which they incur—police and fire protection, traffic engineering, traffic signals, road repair and maintenance. The shortfall is paid for by the property and sales taxpayer (property and sales taxes *are* regressive). Property and sales taxes must include additional increments equivalent to a fuel tax of 40 to 50 cents/gallon for the costs imposed on the community by motorists and the trucking industry. Motorists and truckers, beneficiaries of these services, don't pay for them.

The poor pay both property and sales taxes at much greater proportions of their incomes than do the rest of us. Although the poor are more often renters, the property tax is passed on to them by landlords as a portion of rent. The property tax paid indirectly by the poor as a portion of their rent is not deductible. The "renter's credit," a feature of some state income taxes, cannot always redress the inequity for renters; many poor renters do not pay income tax at all, thus have no access to the partial remedy routinely available to both the middle-class renter and to the homeowner property taxpayer. The property tax is even more regressive than it first appears.

Many of the poor cannot afford automobiles. Even though they pay the taxes which support the automobile/freeway system, they derive no benefit from this portion of their tax burden. On the contrary, as one result of both the diversion of these funds and of trip demand on the freeway system, they suffer the destruction of the public transportation facilities on which they would otherwise depend.

The poor are also deprived of city and county services because of the necessity to spread inadequate local government budgets to cover the needs of motorists and the trucking industry. The budgets for public schools, libraries, mental health services, police and fire protection, the courts, trauma centers, welfare services on which the poor depend disproportionately, are raided to furnish funds for traffic signals, street repair and traffic control.

The poor are more dependent on public schools, police protection and libraries than are the rest of the community. They suffer more from the underfunding of schools and of police departments than do the middle class and the wealthy. The drain on local government funds to fill potholes hurts the poor more than it hurts the rich; the filling of potholes benefits the rich more than it benefits the poor.

The diversion of funds for essential services is a disservice to all citizens, rich and poor alike. The priorities of local government place services to motorists and the trucking industry ahead of schools, police protection and other social services. Traffic signals and parking facilities are accorded higher priority for public funds than are other services to the community.

Retail Prices

The cost of providing free or validated parking is passed-through to shoppers and other clients. This results in an increase of five to fifteen percent in retail and other prices, including those for food and other necessities of life. The poor (and the rest of us) pay these "enhanced" prices—prices which have been increased to cover the cost of parking and other perquisites of the motorist/shopper—even though they (the poor and others) may have walked to the market.

Parking—The Employee Perquisite

"Free" parking at the workplace is an additional drain on the economy. The cost of parking is a corporate deduction; moreover, of course, it is not free. The employer pays, but the cost must either be deducted from the employee's paycheck (which may be decreased five to ten percent) or by increased product prices. Or a combination of both.

There's no free lunch.

Labor unions have found the "free" parking perquisite to be an attractive goal. It is enthusiastically pursued in the collective bargaining process. It is popular with union members because they do not realize that the price is paid in decreased paychecks and/or fewer jobs. The corporate employer has little objection since the cost is fully deductible; at the same time, the benefit to the employee is not regarded as taxable income by the IRS.

Alternative perquisites, such as employer-furnished transit passes or their cash equivalent, are a different matter. The IRS currently permits an untaxed $15 per month transportation allowance to the employee but the prices of monthly bus passes are currently in excess of $40. The real cost of parking, the rental for real estate, improvements and other costs is only infrequently paid by the driver-commuter; it is fully deductible to employers. The subsidy for all parking probably exceeds $10 billion annually for the Los Angeles metropolitan area or roughly $1,000 per year for each driver.

The total of these subsidies to motoring and trucking is the equivalent of a fuel tax increase of $3.50 per gallon. In short, the community as a whole picks up 40% of the cost of operating our automobiles (and an even greater percentage of the cost of trucking) through diversions of portions of the property and sales taxes, through increased retail prices, through decreased paychecks and/or profits amounting to an annual driver's subsidy of $2,400.

Other Effects

Since the automobile is now a necessity, prices in the United States are increased by the need to pay higher wages; each working adult must support a costly vehicle which creates demands for higher salaries and wages. These are passed on to the consumer and have an important impact on prices. The poor also pay these prices.

The Destruction of Transit

These financial externalities create an artificially cheap price for the use of automobiles and trucks, thus making them more attractive than if honest prices prevailed. The result is that public transit, the choice of the poor, is bankrupted for want of ridership. It operates, therefore, at low levels of service. As a consequence, the poor are confined to the ghetto, jobless. Buses are both inadequate and expensive.

Or the poor are required to support automobiles at the cost of as much as 30% of their meager earnings (not merely of the negligible fuel tax) in order to get to work and to participate in urban life.

Our present policies are both foolish and regressive. They favor the middle class and the wealthy because the heavy subsidies for the use of automobiles spare them much of the cost of operating the vehicle. They also deprive the working poor—frequently a member of a racial minority—of acceptable, effective, low-cost transit services. Our system requires that the community support two failed transportation systems—the freeway/automobile system as well as the public transit system—out of the same straitened public purse. This must be the worst of the possible transportation choices.

The "user-pays" principle, despite the protestations of the highway lobby and widespread belief to the contrary, has never been part of the gasoline and automotive taxation policies of the nation. The sum of the fuel tax and the license fee has never been adequate to meet user-costs incurred by government institutions.

Since 1965, inflation has decreased the yield of the fuel tax in adjusted dollars by a factor of four. Although driving has greatly increased, the increased efficiency of automobiles has kept gasoline consumption at about the same level it was in 1965. While inadequate fuel tax yields have been sequestered into trust funds for the construction of urban freeways, property tax yields have had to be increased because inflation made local government's small share of the fuel tax increasingly irrelevant.

A widening gap in city and county budgets was created as inflation increased the cost of services; the gallonage fuel tax remained at about the same low level. The consequence was a substantial shift of the cost of local government from the motorist to the property taxpayer. This shift explains, in large part, California's Proposition 13 "tax revolt" of 1978.

Since the American Petroleum Institute (API) declares that it backs user-pay market principles, we challenge it to support a program to sequester property and sales tax yields to match the sequestration of fuel tax yields.

Such a provision would have two broad provisions: first, that the *only* funds which could be used to pay for *all* services to motorists and to the trucking industry, including automobile-related police and fire protection, traffic control, street repair, *must* be derived from user fees—the fuel tax, the license fee or others. Second, that property tax and sales tax yields must be sequestered to be used *only* for non-automobile related costs such as police and fire protection for non-motorists, support for schools, libraries, parks and civic services. Other provisions to adjust property, sales and fuel tax levels to balance costs would also be included.

The API argument is the cry of the rich on behalf of the poor; a rush to judgment based on conventional wisdom. Both the judgment and the "wisdom" is wildly erroneous.

12

UTILITY AND DISUTILITY

"We now have genuine competition.[*] It may be that Americans must consume less."
                                    —Lester Thurow

Normal supply-and-demand economics have not been permitted to restrain automobile and truck operation in the United States; aberrant economic practices—the free use of roads and parking facilities are the rule of the road. These, plus the high ratio of fixed to marginal costs, encourage excessive use. An honest pricing system should constrain the consumption of scarce and costly resources such as land, infrastructure and fuel.

Roads and parking facilities fill quickly to their capacity because roads and parking spaces appear to be "free" goods. Fuel cost is the only financial constraint on

---

[*] Referring to Japanese and German penetration of world and American markets.

automobile and truck use; fuel is cheap—the price of gasoline in adjusted dollars is lower in 1993 than at any other time in history, one quarter the 1929 price.

Traffic congestion is the real constraint. It creates another phenomenon—"latent demand"—the number of trips that are *not* made because drivers would be subjected to intolerable delay. Such "latent" trips may amount to as much as 30% of existing traffic.

Increasing the capacity of highways in an effort to cope with congestion—widening streets, adding highway lanes, installing timed traffic lights and building more roads—is counterproductive because it results, if anything, in short-term relief only. Because of latent demand, the number of trips increases immediately until the enlarged facility reaches its new capacity.

Congestion returns, perhaps in new locations involving more vehicles. Further, if the project *is* successful in reducing congestion, the reduction creates *"future* latent demand" by encouraging even more home construction on peripheral lands of the urban boundaries. Under existing patterns, automobile use will be increased over the long term, the temporary benefits from the expansion of highway capacity will be nullified. New demands arise for new highway construction in response to new congestion.

The cycle is costly and unproductive, except for those interests which profit from endless road construction and urban sprawl. The community bears the cost; farm land and wilderness disappear beneath asphalt and concrete. Our purpose, the safe flow of people and goods, must be reaffirmed. Road-building should be judged by the same utility criteria we apply (or should apply) to other investments. Moving automobiles has become our purpose.

Vehicles are only tools. Moving people and goods in an expeditious, cost-effective manner need not involve automobiles, trucks or highways. On the contrary, vehicles and infrastructure often comprise an unnecessarily costly, inconvenient system for this purpose.

The following is a measure of the comparative utility and disutility of travel to both the community and the individual traveler.

Safety

Safety is, of course, the most visible of these parameters; the toll is not a trivial matter—45,000 lives lost, 500,000 serious and maiming injuries each year.

The Economy

The economy is also at risk. The nation's economy has declined slowly from the halcyon days following World War II when our nation had the ability to jump-start the economies of the European nations with the $70 billion Marshall Plan. Now we are a debt-ridden shadow of that colossus. The financial hemorrhage and extravagance inherent in our automobile dependence have reduced us to eighth or ninth in an ordered ranking of industrial nations by per capita income. The 25% of GNP spent on all aspects of the automotive/highway sector constitutes an enormous drain of available investment capital.

The nation suffers from competitivitis. For the first time in this century, it confronts a truly competitive world exemplified by the Japanese/German miracle, but other nations have also passed us by. The Japanese are awash in cash; their enterpreneurs do not suffer from a dearth of investment capital. Indeed, many yen, guilders, deutschmark and Swiss francs are invested in the United States because our interest rates have been high and our real estate comparatively cheap.

Environment

By every measure—air pollution, land use, global warming, the consumption of finite resources—the automobile is a major violator; possibly, the greatest abuser of the environment.

Convenience

Convenience must be measured from the standpoint of every type of trip and from everyone's perspective, travelers and non-travelers alike. If excessive automobile use makes it difficult or unsafe to cross streets or to bicycle to work or other destinations, our convenience is reduced.

Land use

The planning of our communities has been taken out of the hands of professional planners because now the developers and politicians make the decisions which shape the community. The loss of friendly neighborhoods and increased alienation result from automobile dependence.

Time

The automobile may or may not offer a faster trip, but none of its occupants will be able to use the time as productively as can passengers on common-carrier systems who have time to read, study or talk with fellow passengers.

Accessibility

The necessity of transit accessibility is the reality for most young, old, poor and handicapped travelers. Although many with wheelchair dependence prefer a fitted van, buses and streetcars are also fitted to accommodate wheelchairs. For others who are handicapped, common carrier transit is the more acceptable. Transit is more accessible to the sight-impaired, for instance, who cannot be accommodated in automobiles unless accompanied by sighted drivers.

User-Friendliness

User-friendliness depends greatly on the user. The macho young man finds automobiles friendlier; his father and mother may be more comfortable on a train than on a freeway. The automobile demands a higher level of personal skills; transit, on the other hand, requires familiarity with protocol.

Reliability

The automobile suffers from a variety of sporadic ailments: dead batteries, flat tires, defective or worn sparkplugs, empty fuel tanks. The trolley car is far more reliable. Since it is obvious that the automobile/highway system does not serve us well, one is tempted to ask "Why have we committed our community so massively to the automobile to the exclusion of other options?"

	Auto	Rail	Weights	Weighted	values
				Auto	Rail
Safety	1	10	10	10	100
Economy	2	7	10	20	70
Environment	1	9	10	10	90
Convenience	8	4	5	40	20
Land-use	2	9	5	10	45
Time	7	6	3	21	18
Accessibility	5	9	3	15	27
User-friendly	5	7	2	10	14
Reliability	2	8	2	4	16
			Totals	140	400

MATRIX - Ranking on a scale of 1 to 10

Both the weighting and the ranking are products of the writers' judgments and they suffer, of course, from personal biases.

Thus the matrix contains a number of defects: it is entirely subjective; there is much overlap; it fails to include pertinent matters such as the future of the world's oil resources; it is concerned only with the individual's transportation needs, not his ego needs. Yet, in all these respects it is conservative and it does offer an approximate guide to the relative merits of available transportation options. Alternative insights and weights are encouraged.

The answer, of course, is that society is not necessarily rational in making such decisions. The nation has contrived a system of incentives applied through distorted market forces. Because these market forces favor the automobile, society is forced to choose the automobile. Thus it is essential to correct our policies so that honest prices and rational market forces can prevail.

Powerful interests wish to maintain the status quo and to expand the automobile/truck sector. Nor are our corporations the only actors; one American in six makes a living manufacturing cars and trucks, repairing them, building the highways and producing or selling oil and its products. These are the factors that tilt the scales heavily in favor of existing patterns.

13

NAÏVE AND DISINGENUOUS SOLUTIONS
Nibbling at the Margins

"The people may be bored with Marxism-Leninism, but they
cling to the safe (if backward) welfare state that Stalinism created."   —Anonymous

The captains of artillery prefer to win the battle with
artillery even though artillery is not always called for.
The following are several of the "solutions" offered by
others to mitigate auto-related problems:

Alternative Fuels

The air pollution problem, which is most visible in Los
Angeles but which is as widespread as Los Angelization,
has generated a multitude of solutions addressed specifically to the problem of smog. Among these programs are

several which would substitute alternative fuels for the prinicipal automotive fuels: gasoline and diesel oil.

Gasoline and diesel oil dominate the transportation market for good reason: they are the commercially available fuels which provide the greatest amount of energy per unit of volume. They are, by far, the cheapest fuel (this may be due, in part, to economies of scale) and are made from a readily available raw material—oil. Oil is as fungible as money. It can be readily and safely stored, shipped easily and cheaply by pipeline, tanker, truck or train.

The market has determined that gasoline and diesel oil are the preferred fuels for the internal combustion engine and for the automobile and truck. Alternatives must either meet the test of lower price and/or greater efficiency and efficacy or they must be imposed on us by government command-and-control strategies.

Methanol

Methanol is the simplest of the alcohols and it is commonly known as "wood" alcohol because it can be made from woody vegetation. Its attraction is that, as a fuel for internal combustion engines, its exhaust gases contain fewer and less objectionable pollutants. It is also toxic and miscible (dissolves readily in water) so its use may incur unacceptable pollution of ground water.

Leaking underground gasoline storage tanks permit gasoline to perculate into the subsoil. Gasoline drops to the top of the water table where it "floats" as a lens on the water. It may impart an odor to ground water where the water table is shallow but is seldom more than a nuisance. Methanol, being toxic and miscible, would be far more objectionable under the same conditions of underground leakage.

Methanol contains about a third less energy per gallon than gasoline. It is corrosive; therefore exposed engine parts—carburetor, injector, tank and fuel lines—must be replaced with corrosion-resistant material, stainless steel.

Methanol can be made from wood or coal. But the most likely method uses methane, natural gas, as the raw material. To substitute methanol for gasoline would require a substantial diversion of natural gas from present uses. While supplies of gas are adequate, diversion of the equivalent of four billion barrels of oil would have a most serious impact on the natural gas market.

The price of the resulting methanol cannot be known at this time. New manufacturing facilities and new storage methods need to be devised and built and the national population of vehicles would need to be retrofitted to use the fuel.

The price of methanol would reflect all these costs so the price would not be less than three to four times the price of the gasoline equivalent. The inevitable increase in the price of natural gas stemming from this increased demand must also be reckoned in considering the comparative cost of methanol as an alternative fuel. How then can drivers and the community to be persuaded to substitute methanol for gasoline? By government fiat?

The benefit of the methanol substitution for motor fuel would be a marginal improvement in the quality of air for American cities. Since this is a benefit enjoyed by the community as a whole, it is not the lone driver who must make the choice and pay the price. Methanol's contribution of carbon dioxide to global warming would be greater than that of gasoline.

Ethanol

Ethanol is the familiar "grain" alcohol of beer, wine and whiskey. It is not toxic as is methanol but it is miscible. In Brazil, where it is made from sugar cane at a substantial financial cost over gasoline it has been marketed commercially for over a decade. Special manufacturing, storage facilities and retrofitted vehicles are required throughout the country.

Depending on the raw material used to manufacture ethanol, global warming gases as well as air pollution would be reduced. The energy content is less than that of gasoline. The cost in Brazil is cheaper than imported gasoline since gasoline must be paid for in hard foreign currency, but the cost to the population is severe. The poor can no longer count on cheap staple foods because so much land is devoted to sugar cane production for this purpose.

Hydrogen

Hydrogen can be used as a motor fuel. It is highly desirable from the air quality point of view since its exhaust would be water vapor and the oxides of nitrogen. But it is inherently expensive financially and energy-wise. The production of hydrogen gas requires the input of more energy than can be derived as output from its consumption.

The effect of hydrogen on global warming depends on the type of energy which would be used to manufacture the gas. If it is to be oil or coal or other hydrocarbons, the impact on global warming will be greater than that of the continued use of gasoline and diesel fuel. Greenhouse gases, air pollution and acid rain will be emitted at the factory where the hydrogen is manufactured, instead of at the vehicle.

The substitution of hydrogen requires a huge cost for storage and manufacturing facilities plus the conversion of vehicles. Hydrogen is dangerous, it must be stored in absorption in special compounds to avoid hazard to the driver, passengers and the community.

Electric Cars

Electric cars are powered by batteries and burn no gasoline so no pollution is emitted by the vehicle. The electrical energy is produced at a central power station using oil, coal or nuclear fuel. A "hybrid" car is also proposed which would employ a small internal combustion engine to extend its range.

Air pollutants would still be produced in the process of producing electricity but these would be emitted at the power plant. The quantity of pollutants is uncertain—they might be either greater or less. Air quality might be considerably improved, compared with that produced by equivalent internal combustion engines, but that depends on a number of unresolved factors.

It is an attractive, clean, quiet and simple vehicle needing no transmission or clutch. Tune-ups, carburetors, distributors, timing-belt adjustments, anti-freeze, radiators, and a other worries associated with automobiles would vanish.

The intrinsic difficulty is the necessity to store energy in the form of electricity within the vehicle—a problem which has not yielded, as yet, to technology. Despite intensive research, the only practical, commercial technology remains the lead-acid battery—the battery in your car.

These batteries are heavy and the energy needs of the automobile are roughly proportional to its weight. Thus, increasing energy storage capacity aboard the vehicle consumes more energy and imposes the necessity of providing more energy capacity in the vehicle.

In other words, because the vehicle expends a great amount of energy in transporting its stored energy, its energy requirements soon reach a steep peak without producing better performance, increasing range or other beneficial results. Resolution of this design conundrum will not be easy. A breakthrough in battery design is possible, though not probable in the short term. In addition, these batteries must be replaced every two to three years—an expenditure of several thousand dollars per change.

Amory Lovins has suggested the design of a commercially attractive automobile using a radically different approach. His design would use a molded plastic chassis and body to reduce weight, a combined power train comprising a small battery, regenerative braking and a high-speed flywheel/generator/motor which, if carefully designed, might be capable of storing energy with a low weight/kilowatt ratio. Solar panels can be used to extend the range of the vehicle.

The best that serious design efforts have produced to this date (including regenerative braking, possible only in an electric car) is a vehicle costing $25,000 which can travel 120 miles on a charge and which requires an hours-long rest period for recharging. This vehicle may be adequate for many needs; however, it would not be the best choice for a skiing vacation. It does not appear to be commercially viable if it is to compete freely with gasoline-powered vehicles in the market.

With respect to air pollution, the battery-powered automobile would be inferior to rail transit, since the energy requirements for electric automobiles would be greater than for gasoline-powered cars. Rail vehicles are not required to carry their own energy. The disposal of batteries is also an environmental hazard, although strict regulation and recycling lead and other components may be profitable.

The crucial matters of gridlock, death-in-the-streets and public and private cost would not be mitigated by the substitution of electrically driven automobiles. If present levels of automobile use are inevitable, the electric automobile may have a place in transportation.

Our premise is that the flow of people and goods is the problem that must be addressed. And if full-cost pricing is adopted (all costs associated with auto use would be paid by users), the entire paradigm of the indispensable automobile might well be discarded.

When that occurs, the substitution of the electric automobile would depend on its viability in the marketplace.

High Occupancy Vehicles (HOVs)

The conventional wisdom is that, by increasing the average number of passengers occupying the automobiles on the freeways, we can reduce the number of trips. It is believed that this must be useful in reducing congestion and air pollution. This view is optimistic. There are two reasons, rooted in economic principle, for our pessimism.

- The first is the corruption of the pricing system by which the commuter is deceived as to the financial cost of car commuting.

Sunk Costs — The large out-of-pocket costs of owning a car are "sunk costs," that is, the costs of depreciation and insurance do not increase whether the car is driven five miles or 50,000.

Deferred Costs — Repairs, tires and maintenance which increase with the miles, are "deferred costs"—the driver is not really aware of these costs—tires are replaced at two to four year intervals, for instance. The driver does not recognize these as "marginal" costs—the financial costs that increase with driving.

Subsidized Costs — Parking at work, shopping and elsewhere is generally a perquisite furnished by employer or shop; the cost of parking at home is included in the cost of the mortgage or rent. The use of the highway is also "free." The costs of traffic signals, street repair, police and fire protection—all of which are essential to the driver—are believed by the public to be subsumed in the gasoline tax. In fact, most local government transportation-related costs are paid for by property and sales taxes.

What, then, remains of market constraints—the marginal costs—which inform the driver much the trip is costing him financially? The only constraint that remains is the cost of fuel. Both the gasoline tax and the total price of gasoline in adjusted dollars are lower than at any time in the history of the automobile. The cost of gasoline for a normal commute might be "seen" as about 85¢, less than bus fare.

Why should a commuter give up the comfort, privacy, status and authority provided by the automobile? Certainly not because of financial costs.

We might be tempted to say this person should carpool because it is in the interest of the community to reduce traffic congestion and air pollution. In *The Tragedy of the Commons*, Garrett Hardin tells us why neither you nor anyone else will respond cheerfully to that suggestion. Most of us see, all too clearly, that it is not in our personal interest to voluntarily give up our automobile to benefit the community. In a city in which 40 million trips are made daily by automobile, the reduction of two trips per day returns to the commuter the benefit of a sacrificed trip divided by 20 million. Not an attractive option.

Nor is that all.

- There is a second reason. The *aggravation and loss of time* due to traffic congestion is a cost, albeit not a financial cost, perceived by the commuter. If this driver has reason to believe that congestion will be encountered the driver may adopt other means of getting to work.

By diverting single drivers to carpools, the cars of the carpoolers no longer create air-pollution and congestion; their absence provides vacancies and "free-flow" in the freeway lanes. This is the reason, after all, that the encouragement of HOVs seems, at first glance, to be an attractive program.

Congestion, therefore, is essential to encourage carpooling. What happens when the congestion is gone? Carpooling does not have inherent charms to attract commuters. Carpooling, after all, is like a one bus busline.

Finding they are no longer hampered by congestion, other drivers come to fill the vacant spaces. This is the "latent" demand already described. This puts us back to square one—congested. Except, in addition, we now have an HOV lane with a number of carpools.

And, if that were not enough, the creation of "freeflow" on our freeways would, in time, generate *future latent demand*"—the displacement of middle-class housing even farther out on the periphery of our urban areas where land is cheap—thus creating more transportation demand and demand for increasing highway capacity.

HOVs and HOV lanes (assuming they are effective in attracting carpooling commuters) will, like all other methods which increase highway capacity (including TSM, Smart Streets, Congestion Pricing and the construction of new highways), have the effect of generating new demand for more travel.

Like the Sorcerer's Apprentice, we are caught up in an endless round of, first, increasing travel demand and, second, the implementation of project/programs, including HOV programs and new freeway construction. The intention, of course, is to furnish the means to satisfy the new demand. We build new highways, widen old ones, make our highways more efficient; that is the traditional, obvious response. But, since these measures actually *increase* demand for travel, they cannot satisfy that demand.

Congestion Pricing

The Congestion Pricing concept originated with transportation economists who reason that, since we have invested such huge sums in the highway system of the nation, we should do what can be done to make that system as efficient as possible. Within this narrow paradigm, their proposal makes some sense. They would require that vehicles be equipped with Automatic Vehicle Identification (AVI) devices and at relevant locations the highway network would be equipped with "readers" which, aided by the vehicle-mounted AVI responders, would identify the users recording place and time. A billing system would debit fees from a pre-paid account established by the vehicle owner.

This debited fee would vary; where the location is congested and the time is within the "rush" hour period, the fee would be greater. At other times and locales, the fee might be less. The driver would, thereby, be encouraged to use more appropriate routes and times of day. An alternative system, instead of debiting a pre-paid account, would be to bill the driver (or vehicle owner) by means of a monthly bill similar to the telephone bill.

There is little doubt that the goals of the economist-protagonists could be achieved. But are these goals useful? Creating more efficiency is like building new highway capacity; it would simply encourage more driving. The bottom line would be more trips and congestion at different locations.

One side-effect would result from implementation— the problem of the parallel free highway. With Congestion Pricing in place, we can expect parallel roadways to be more congested during the "expensive" hours which would require that readers be installed on the parallel roadways as well.

Protagonists are attracted to the idea because it is an "elegant" solution to the problem of the congested highway. More efficient highways, however, mean that the use of costly cars and trucks will be encouraged at the expense of patronage for the less costly and more efficient rail transit and rail freight systems. Thus, more efficient highways can mean less efficient transportation.

The benefits could be marginally useful, depending on the magnitude of the fees and on how the community perceives the benefits. Mitigation of congestion would be temporary at best. The freeways would be congested during longer periods—perhaps during the entire day, not alone at "rush hour."

Congestion Pricing seems to discard an advantage. A better use of costly AVI equipment—which would definitely justify its expense—would be to charge a rational level of rent for the use of highway and parking facilities. This would require the installation of more "readers," increasing the cost somewhat—society's benefits would be far greater.

Transportation System Management (TSM)

TSM is jargon for the assortment of procedures and devices such as HOVs, HOV lanes, ramp metering and synchronized traffic signals which are intended to relieve congestion by making the freeways and arterials more efficient.

Ramp metering is something of a mystery. These are signals installed at the juncture of on-ramps and free-ways which "meter" the vehicles entering the freeway from the ramps. By forcing the vehicles to stop briefly and permitting them to proceed only at timed intervals, it is apparently thought that the turbulence in traffic flow imposed by the entering vehicles can be reduced or avoided.

By requiring the cars to stop, the queue of entering cars is spaced at intervals by the meter. The cars must then accelerate to reach the speed of the outside traffic lane. Many of these vehicles, having entered that lane, will then migrate across the intervening lanes to the inside, high speed lane.

It would seem that their benefits to traffic flow are questionable; they may occur at certain levels of flow, they are probably neither beneficial nor detrimental at other levels. Our observations indicate that turbulence induced by metered on-ramp traffic is still a factor in producing congestion.

Synchronized traffic signals are believed to produce traffic flow on arterials with fewer interruptions. They are an important addition to the tools employed by TSM.

The conventional wisdom is that they reduce frustration, congestion and emissions from stop-and-go acceleration. They are also expensive, requiring computers, networks of radio, cable links and other connectors.

Ramp meters and synchronized traffic signals, like all methods which improve highway capacity (if they produce any results at all), will have the same effect. They will encourage more traffic. Latent demand is waiting in the wings to fill the highways. Congestion would still plague the freeways and arterials, but at greater numbers of cars and drivers. None of these methods can produce beneficial results so long as the use of highway and parking facilities is a "free" good.

Smart Streets

The widely admired Smart Streets programs are aimed, like Congestion Pricing and TSM concepts, only at the problem of traffic congestion. They are to provide the motorist early warning of congestion with alternative, convenient routes suggested around the congested freeway using side streets, arterials or possibly other freeways. Information would flow to a central office from a network of sensors which would signal constricted traffic flow and in turn be broadcast to all vehicles entering the congested area. It is implicit, of course, that excess capacity is available on the parallel roadways expected to double as convenient detours. To be fully effective the Smart Streets project must, of necessity, include these roadways in its sensor network. In short, the entire road system surrounding major arterials would have to be provided with congestion sensors.

Variants of the Smart Streets proposal would provide this warning either by means of a dashboard mounted CRT screen (plus a specialized computer and a radio-link furnished at owner expense) or by electronic signboards installed at intervals at roadside. Smart Streets, like Congestion Pricing, proposes to provide the required additional highway capacity by making existing roadway networks more efficient.

But, like all other proposals which depend on an increase in highway efficiency or highway capacity, Smart Streets have a significant flaw. This is the implicit belief that travel demand is an "independent variable," to borrow a phrase from mathematicians. In other words, protagonists of Smart Streets believe the numbers of trips generated by a population of people and automobiles will increase at rates projected from past experience, regardless of whatever else is done.

The most important constraint on driving, given the existing state of the pricing distortion, is traffic congestion. Since driving is viewed by the driver as "free," the demand for trips is almost infinite. Provide relief for congestion and you get more trips, not congestion relief; the result of Smart Streets will be more traffic congestion, more air pollution in more places—and all at greater expense to the community. The other impacts of the automobile syndrome would be vastly exacerbated— we would have escalated the problem in the worst way possible.

Telecommuting

Telecommuting would allow some workers to remain at home at least part of the work week, provided the nature of their work permits. Each would thus save two trips a day. Employees using computers, fax machines and telephones may be able to be as effective working at home.

Many jobs, however, require personal and physical interaction with others—not the least, of course, being the need to reassure the boss the worker is producing. Some employees may have travel needs unrelated to work, which may be made the more pressing by the fact that they remain in their homes during normal working hours. Many people need the stimulus provided by interaction with other workers. A small portion of the working population would probably find it possible to conduct their business from their homes; some would find it attractive, especially those with responsibilities for small children.

Unfortunately, the trips which are saved by this practice would probably not benefit the community by reducing traffic congestion and air pollution. Latent demand would tend to refill the freeways and arterials. Telecommuting would mitigate congestion and pollution for awhile but its bottom line is likely to be marginal. The investment, which would have to be made by employers and employees alike, may not result in benefits to those who invest. How can they then be persuaded to make the investment?

Conclusion

These solutions are implicitly justified on the grounds that alternatives to the automobile are unacceptable. This also argues that present levels of automobile use are immutable.

Many transit systems—San Francisco's Bay Area Rapid Transit, the San Diego Trolley, the light-rail Blue Line between Los Angeles and Long Beach—have successfully weaned people from automobiles. Each has demonstrated considerable acceptance among automobile owners even though the subsidies—the free use of highways, of parking facilities and of local government services—still exist and present highly unfavorable financial incentives.

Since automobile use is heavily subsidized, real transit patronage preferences have yet to be determined. Withdrawal of the subsidies would do more to mitigate congestion and all other automobile problems than any of these costly projects. Real solutions, therefore, are those which would correct the pricing corruption that characterizes the transportation problem and perpetuates both excessive automobile use and the myth of public preference for automobiles.

Responsible pricing would authenticate the consumer's "dollar-vote" for it would result in the mitigation of our transportation problems. Continued reliance on naive approaches will perpetuate the sins of the past: increasing congestion, air pollution, acid rain, the risk of global warming and ozone depletion, excessive cost and the waste of resources.

Bureaucrats, politicians and vested interests have been permitted to make critical decisions. Instead, it is the market which must do this for us. We must demand that market principles be applied to transportation. Nibbling at the margins of the problem will not save us; the deck chairs should be rearranged *after* the ship has been saved.

14

WHAT IS TO BE DONE?

"Sometimes we must do what is required."

—Winston Churchill

Solutions will not be easy; over the years the automobile has entrenched itself in our economy, in our psyches and in our physical surroundings. Nevertheless, solutions are inevitable; they are necessary to our continued economic and environmental health. Timing is the only question.

The only real remedy is the correction of the cost/price distortion which would be in the long-term interest of everyone—drivers and non-drivers alike. In the short-term, however, there would be some withdrawal symptoms. The one American in six who works in the automobile/truck/highway sector would be unhappy. The working poor, who must depend in the short-term on gas guzzlers, would have reason to complain. The problem is complicated politically because conventional wisdom has been so badly distorted; we are poorly informed as to our relationship with the automobile and its economic impact.

We now have no mechanism to adjust price to be commensurate with cost. Because so much of the cost of driving is subsidized, we have been forced into a circle of distorted prices, almost infinite trip demand and the futile construction of more highways.

The Law of Supply and Demand is fully as intractable as the physical laws. We cannot fool Mother Nature. Consumption of goods and services varies inversely with marginal costs as seen by the consumer. The marginal cost of automobile use is absurdly low. Elimination of subsidies and the conversion of "fixed" costs to "marginal" costs are indispensable.

The First Alternative: An Increased Fuel Tax

The least costly means of mitigation would be a substantially increased fuel tax, as revenue-neutral as is feasible. The yield from this increase should, concurrently, be used to eliminate or reduce the property tax, the sales tax or the social security tax—all regressive taxes.

Under this regime, we estimate that the fuel tax would have to be increased to between five and nine dollars per gallon at current levels of consumption. This increase would be necessary if users are to pay the total cost of highway and parking facilities through an increased fuel tax. The lower figure is our rough estimate of the effect of reducing the financial externalities alone; the larger figure is the effect of reducing both the financial and the environmental externalities. Moreover, since the effect of this increase would be a marked decrease in the consumption of gasoline, the tax may have to be adjusted to even higher levels in the future.

The increase in the fuel tax should be "revenue-neutral" for three reasons: such an increase, without a concurrent decrease in the financial impacts on the middle class, would be politically unacceptable. Secondly, the question of equity must be resolved, at least partially; this can be done only by reducing the tax burdens on the poor and on non-drivers. And, finally, financial contraints on local and other government spending must be maintained. At the same time, measures should be taken to ensure that essential services are not starved of funds as they are at present.

While the burden shifts to the wallets of drivers, the poor would still be paying retail prices swollen by the cost of parking (the cost of employer-furnished free parking can be "cashed-out," thus abolishing that portion of the problem). The inequity inherent in increased retail prices would be partially balanced by the tax shift. The resultant balance, though imperfect, would still be a vast improvement over the huge inequity of current price corruption.

The Second Alternative:
Automatic Vehicle Identification (AVI)

The Automatic Vehicle Identification system is the more sophisticated alternative; it would directly charge those who use the roads and/or parking facilities. AVI permits the assessment of user fees based on defined costs. It would be more equitable than a fuel tax increase.

Sensors, either buried in the pavement or placed in visual readers, would identify transponders carried by passing vehicles. The transponders can be mounted in the license plate or in a small key-card placed in the windshield. The system senses and records the location and time of each vehicle's passage.

Because it can identify vehicles as they incur costs, the AVI system has a considerable advantage over the fuel tax. It is independent of the nature of the fuel; it could be used to selectively charge by routes and/or times of travel in order to mitigate peak-period congestion and it could be used to charge for parking in both public and private parking facilities, including on-street parking spaces (eliminating meters and meter-readers). It could also be used to apply disincentives to abusive drive-through and spill-over parking on residential streets and other aberrant behavior. Free market forces would painlessly persuade drivers to use their vehicles in the fairest, most efficient manner.

AVI could also be used to collect automobile insurance premiums, billing the user on a mileage basis. Thus, the cost of insurance would be effectively converted from a "fixed" cost to a "marginal" cost.

Another possibility made feasible by AVI would be the substitution of car rental for car ownership. Cars could be rented either on a mileage or an hourly basis or on a combination. This would present both drivers and the business world with an interesting range of options. Instead of selling cars, car dealers could rent them, much as rental firms do today, except that the practice would be vastly expanded. Rental dealers would compete as they do now: on price.

The driver would be freed from the burden of owning a car and free also to choose his identity, whether to be the macho, the dandy or the careful middle-class citizen. If he must have a car for tonight's date, for instance, the rental dealer could be instructed to send a Porsche; if to be used for tomorrow's sales campaign, a Cadillac might be the choice. If a family camping trip is planned, an RV could be selected. If a skiing trip, a four-wheel drive vehicle equipped with ski-rack and snow tires. The embarrassment of installing tire chains in icy weather could be avoided.

If the driver's objective is transportation at the least expense, an inexpensive, compact car could be chosen. In short, the widest possible range of transportation options would be possible. Furthermore, almost all costs of vehicle use would be at the "margin," none would remain in the "fixed" cost category. Freedom to choose would provide efficient, less costly travel.

The mental burden of maintenance and repair, dealing with acquisitive mechanics and body-and-fender repair men, the unpleasant chore of believing improbable "diagnoses" would be left to professionals and to dealers. Automobiles would no longer be attractive accessories to criminal acts. Widespread auto theft would become a memory. Instant identity would have a salutary effect.

Family vehicles would no longer be the rule; the adolescent in the household would not be as compelled to wheedle and whinge the family car for the Saturday night date. The driver's license would no longer be regarded as a rite of passage. The consequence would be better familial discipline, lower death rates among 16- to 24-year-olds and a less frenzied journey to adulthood.

Driving would be the more enjoyable because the vehicle could be intelligently chosen; the highways would be tranquil, safer. The driver would put more money in the bank because there would no longer be the requirement to invest capital in the purchase of vehicles. Expenses would be closely tailored to desires and needs.

Of the alternative modes of collecting user-fees, the AVI is the more costly. The installation of sensors, the outfitting of 180 million vehicles with transponders, the maintenance of sensors, the billing infrastructure and its operation, would be expensive. Fuel taxes are in place; their implementation would be easy and cheap.

Mitigation of Parking Subsidies

The cost of parking should be paid for by the consumer-driver. Only in this way can the knowledge, necessary to permit rational choices, of actual costs be made available to the driver. In this way options, alternative modes can become available. "Free" parking should no longer be used to subsidize driving.

Under the gentle pressure of environmental laws, political leaders are beginning to react positively to the "free" parking syndrome. The California State Legislature and the Los Angeles City Council will soon consider legislation to help correct this aberration; employers would be required to determine the real cost to them of the parking perquisite and offer their employees the cash equivalent of this cost; this is called "cashing-out."

Mitigation of free parking for the shopper, which is more important as an incentive, is also more difficult. It may be that the increased fuel tax and its reduction of regressive taxes must be relied upon, for want of a better strategy. An AVI strategy would be precise, effective.

Public and private subsidies, in addition to the inequitable treatment of non-drivers, are also unfair to drivers, because they give a false signal (that driving is inexpensive). Drivers are, therefore, unable to make rational choices with regard to travel. Both government and private institutions subsidize the use of automotive vehicles. The relevant government policies, aside from the provision of free highway use and free government services, are the zoning and taxing practices which create these subsidies.

Private subsidies are the provision of free or validated parking for employees and clients. "Free" parking, of course, is costly. It is provided by business firms because of competitive pressures. The supply of parking spaces is continually increased with the construction of new buildings by requirements of local building regulations.

The cost of parking is currently absorbed in the cost of doing business and finds its way into the prices of goods and services purchased by consumers—whether or not they drive to the place of business. In addition, business firms as contributors through general taxation channels, already pass other portions of highway cost on to consumers and employees in the form of decreased wages or increased prices for goods and services.

The incorporation of parking spaces into building code requirements has the effect of inexorably increasing the number of parking spaces. Thus, prices for parking are decreased because the supply has been increased.

Mitigating the Effect of Fixed Costs

The automobile's high ratio of fixed costs to marginal costs is another incentive to drive. Purchase and financing costs, insurance premiums, registration and license fees are "fixed" costs which do not vary with the use of the vehicle. They are the greatest portion of automotive costs.

Tires, maintenance and repairs increase with vehicle use, but the driver is confronted with these "deferred" costs at month- or year-long intervals, not daily or weekly; they do not function as marginal cost constraints.

The cost of fuel, encountered weekly is the only "marginal" cost which affects the driver's decision to drive. But the cost of fuel in the United States is almost negligible compared to the magnitude of other costs. Although drivers perceive the cost of fuel, perhaps 85¢, as the cost of an urban trip, the actual cost, shared with the community, may be as much as ten dollars. Once the vehicle has been purchased, fixed costs compel the owner to use it. The more driving, the less the per-mile costs of depreciation and insurance. Per-mile fixed costs cannot be reduced by leaving the car in the driveway. To minimize this effect, fixed costs should be converted to mileage-related costs.

For example, automobile insurance could be paid for at the gas pump as an impost on the cost of fuel. The yield would cover the costs for "PL&PD" (public liability and property damage) claims for the those cars registered within a political subdivision—census tract, zip code, city or county. Insurance coverage for each subdivision could be let by contract through a bidding procedure. Bidding would be permitted by pre-qualified insurance carriers only. Adjustment for unusual risk exposure—a poor driving record or age-related risks—would be handled in the registration and driver's license process. Drivers could obtain additional desired coverage such as "collision, comprehensive, fire and theft" by purchasing it separately at agents at competitive market rates.

PPN : Pay at the pump, Private, No fault

The motorist would benefit in several ways, "uninsured motorist" premiums would no longer be necessary, "redlining" would vanish, the overall cost of insurance would decrease substantially (administrative and sales costs would be reduced, traffic density and traffic accidents would decrease). Every driver would be automatically insured; the victims of traffic accidents would be assured of coverage. The benefits to society would be more substantial than our cursory examination indicates.

Registration and license fees could be collected in a similar manner. Even the purchase and financing charges for the vehicle could be paid for as mileage rather than as a consequence of ownership. This would be more feasible using the AVI system, although it could also be done with the aid of sealed odometers; depreciation of the car could be determined by mileage as well as, or instead of, the age of the vehicle. By abolishing public and private subsidies and by rectifying the fixed/marginal cost relationship, drivers could obtain far better control of expenses, reducing them to desired levels. Marketplace economics, applied to the remainder of our economy, brought to the automotive sector would benefit both driver and community. Equity would also be served by relieving the non-driver of the burden of these costs.

Pedestrian Rights

The automobile is now given priority. Even if motorists and the trucking industry pay rational tolls for the use of the streets, thereby establish legitimate rights to their use, each individual, whether riding, bicycling or afoot, should have an equal right, with equal safety, to use the public streets and roads.

The automobile should take a back seat to human needs. The public street must be truly public, available for free, regulated passage of everyone, whether driver or non-driver. Since the driver has chosen the option of imposing a substantive hazard on others, the burden should be his.

Jaywalking laws should be adjusted to provide greater convenience for pedestrians. Compelling pedestrians to go to a far corner before crossing a street cannot be equitable. Furthermore, the sanctity of the crosswalk must be rigorously enforced. Although these supposedly assure a measure of safety, the safety is often a tragic illusion. Rights must be properly protected for all, not only for those in automobiles.

Persons at the wheel should (although they usually do not) remember that, in the next moment, they will be afoot trying to cross the street, waiting for a benevolent driver to provide that privilege. Even as they hurtle along, some family member may be elsewhere trying to cross a street in safety.

Conclusion

Were these reforms to be put in place, no one would be financially worse off; on the contrary, the effect of the change would be to *reduce* the cost of living. Citizens would have new options permitting them to limit their expenses by reducing automobile use. The tax shift would provide new incentives to combine trips, carpool, use public transit and relocate homes and businesses to minimize driving.

Weaning drivers from highway welfare, placing them on a self-supporting, freemarket footing, would also decrease costs of local government bureaucracies which are heavily weighted with automobile-related services. Transportation efficiency would be enhanced; pressures to build more urban freeways would vanish.

By increasing transit ridership, the efficiency and service levels of public transit facilities would be greatly increased, thereby enhancing transit viability and accelerating the construction of new projects. It would also reduce the huge public subsidies now necessary to permit them to survive but which also keep them functioning at present low service levels.

The diversion of general funds for the benefit of highway users must be stopped. This would complement existing laws which sequester fuel tax funds, permiting their use only for highway construction and maintenance. Existing laws do not stop the flow of funds from federal, state and local governments to pay for highway-related expenses.

The principle that general funds should not be diverted to pay for the costs of highways should be incorporated in the law. These prohibited costs should include but not be restricted to rights-of-way, construction, maintenance, policing, traffic signals, crossing guards, drainage, landscaping and noise abatement.

Equitable property taxes on the real estate should also be levied; this would be highly controversial since title to the property resides in the community. However, if the use of highway rights-of-way is to be consistent with other uses of real property, the tax on rights-of-way should be legitimized, levied and paid by the driver-beneficiary. The highway yield should, like other property tax yields, go to the general fund to be used for the general support of non-automobile-related services to the community.

Since we lack satisfactory transportation alternatives in most American cities, it is argued that, because drivers have no option, they should not be forced to pay increased user fees. It is said to be unfair; tax-shift changes should be delayed to await the reconstruction of transit facilities.

This is a chicken and egg situation; the construction of rail transit facilities requires significant investments in capital, time and rights-of-way. Experience tells us that the acceleration of transit investment and construction will not take place until we see a dramatic increase in the demand for transit ridership. That will require a level playing-field.

The driver currently rides cheaply on the backs of the taxpaying and retail price-paying public; public transit has been left to die on the vine. If American society continues to subsidize the automobile, the free market can never work its magic. Terminating the subsidies and requiring the automobile to stand on its own wheels will restore profitability to public transit and make its service once more attractive to travelers and to private investors. It will also make automobile and truck driving much safer, less stressful and more enjoyable. And it will do this without the construction of new highways.

The adoption of free market principles will, no doubt, cause serious dislocations. Any massive change in these pricing relationships must be made gradually; it should be made over an extended transitional period, say five to ten years. Road users must be given the opportunity to become acclimated to paying increasing portions of the costs that they generate.

Although it would be convenient if public transit facilities could be built and become operative before the cost of automobile use descends fully upon the automobile user's shoulders, it is physically and politically impossible. Because of the great annual cost of the existing pricing system to the nation, however, the process must move along as quickly as possible.

There is little probability that these proposals will be quickly embraced. Like so many other necessary and appropriate concepts, their adoption will be opposed and postponed by the difficulties of the real world.

One in every six workers in the nation is employed in an auto-related occupation. Large vested interests profit from automobile dependency; they will not gladly give up their advantage. Bureaucrats who work in related fields will defend their tax-supported empires. These individuals and corporations will defend their jobs, their careers and their profits just as their counterparts do during the transition process in Russia.

Changes in the means by which we pay for the use of our automobiles are essential if our automobile-dependency is to be mitigated and equity restored. Human beings must reclaim their dominance over the automobile; sensible priorities must prevail.

When we put aside myth and denial in honest devotion to our own interests, to the cause of rational government, efficient transportation and the free marketplace, it will then be possible to resolve these issues.

15

EPILOGUE

"There's something wrong with treating the earth as though it was a business in liquidation."

—Herman Daly, economist, World Bank

". . . Economist's accounting framework, and the models built on it, assigns no economic value to changes in natural resource stocks. This basic measuring instrument must be recalibrated if policymakers are to recognize and be held accountable for the wholesale disruption of natural systems now under way. . . . [The depreciation of capital assets] is written off . . . against the value of production. . . . This practice recognizes that consumption cannot be maintained . . . simply by drawing down the stock of capital without replenishing it. Natural resource assets, however, are not so valued."   —Robert Repetto

". . . One pervasive myth must be squelched—that environmental protection hurts the economy." —Amory Lovins, Joseph Romm

We have deliberately focussed our argument on financial and economic costs because there is, presently, little

165

recognition of their magnitude and because these considerations are often the more persuasive. It is obvious that there are other costs, particularly environmental costs.

Environmental externalities are difficult (if not impossible) to evaluate and/or quantify in financial terms. There is no market, therefore no price, for clean air, for an atmosphere free of ozone depletion and the threat of global warming, for sustainable energy supplies, for cities free of traffic congestion, traffic accidents and their victims.

As we have written elsewhere, the subsidies we provide motorists and the trucking industry exceed $400 billion annually. Because a trip by car or truck is at least four times as costly as a trip by rail, the subsidies are not an adequate measure of economic waste. We estimate that economic inefficiencies due to automotive dependency probably exceed $700 billion.

This figure explains why, since the mid-60s, American goods have had difficulty competing with those of competing industrial economies. Since there is no free lunch, our transportation waste and excessive costs are inexorably reflected in the prices of our products. In addition failure to generate capital because of inadequate personal savings is also reflected in American industry's inability to invest sufficiently to maintain productivity growth and to generate new jobs.

Lest there be misunderstanding of the magnitude of the figure for subsidies, $400 billion annual costs translates roughly into a five-dollars-per-gallon increase in the fuel tax (or $6.25 gasoline). If we are also to collect for an equivalent of the environmental externalities the fuel tax increase would be more like nine dollars per gallon.

By correcting these market abuses, we can have it both ways: we can enjoy the fruits of a healthier environment for ourselves and our children. We can also relish a return to a healthier and more competitive economy.

Other Thoughts

Where we find environmental abuse, we invariably find that it is caused by prostitution of market forces. If not by corruption of price through subsidies or otherwise, then through the neglect or understatement of environmental values.

Genuine free markets must honestly communicate the full cost of the product to the consumer. Where this principle is violated, critical interests of the community are damaged; we believe that it is violated more often than not.

The Marketplace

To many, the word "market" has an ominous ring. Not without reason. The marketplace is often used by uninformed ideologues to justify profitable, but destructive policies.

The market needs no advocate. We have no choice as to whether it is to be invoked. Like the force of gravity, market forces are always present. Our options consist only of choosing whether these forces are to be used honestly for the common good. The market must be purged of inaccurate information. Prices must reflect full cost of resource exploitation including considerations of sustainability.

At the same time, markets must not be permitted to create egregious side-effects. These two purposes, in the short term, are often mutually exclusive. How does one protect the farmer while removing his subsidies? Not without difficulty.

We remind the reader that, if he drops an object, it will fall to the floor. If the price of a commodity is artificially lowered by a subsidy, that commodity will be produced and consumed to excess. Just as we recognize and accommodate the force of gravity, we must recognize and respect market forces; we must also take care that they serve us well.

Adverse Possession

There is no market, therefore no price, for the most valuable resources of the planet. How much real utility is lost to each of us when our supply of clean water is polluted, when our air is laced with carcinogens, when the wetlands and the forests of the earth are destroyed? Do we, as individuals, have a property right in these resources?

Of course we do.

This "property right" is similar to that (known in legalese as "adverse possession") which belongs to habitual, overt users of land or water. When property or water from a stream has been used "notoriously" (in the sense of "openly") for a substantial period of time, the user can claim a right under the law to its use in perpetuity. Since all human beings can argue that they have a history of the notorious use of clean air, clean water, clean oceans, and healthy, operative forests, they can, by the same principle, claim a property right to the undisturbed use of these resources.

But these property rights are not now reinforced by tradition, by past practice or by definitive provisions of law. Are these rights any the less real because of this lack?

Of course not.

Are they not protected by the "natural law" invoked recently by the conservative side in the course of the Robert Bork and Clarence Thomas hearings?

Of course they are.

Although we cannot profit from the sale of these rights, they are property rights nonetheless. Furthermore, we can usefully establish a price for each such right; we can assess the value of our enjoyment of these resources.

Consensual Pricing

"Consensual pricing" asks the consumer his assessment of value. When we wish to know the price we should place on clean air, we must ask the public what it believes that clean air should be worth. The asking must use scientific polling techniques.

Is clean air worth 50¢ per day to each of us; our guess is that it is worth at least that amount. When multiplied by 15 million, the population of the Los Angeles Basin, for instance, the total cost of foul air to Los Angelenos amounts to $7,500,000 per day or $2.74 billion per year. That could become the price to be assessed in the form of fees based on the proportion contributed by each polluter and paid to the community for the right to pollute.

Not a precise method, but far better than nothing. Our present situation, for practical purposes, is "nothing."

Jobs and Jobs and Jobs

Full employment and prosperity are the Holy Grail of all politicians. None of the governments, among all the nations of the world which make this promise, are capable of fulfilling it.

The Bush expedition to Japan, trailing chief executives of the Big Three auto makers, was an election year ploy, a display intended to demonstrate to voters the Administration's great concern for the prosperity of the American working man. The result was pure Gilbert & Sullivan; the overpaid, loss-making CEOs provided a slapstick chorus of whining complaint. The President's ill-timed attack of stomache-flu added the ultimate comic touch.

The Bush trip embarrassed Americans. It demonstrated American impotence when confronted with the economic power of Japanese industry. We were Little Leaguers, our bumbling father trying to persuade the fathers of the dominant team to allow us to win, if only once in awhile.

Are Americans suffering from Japanese manipulation of factors bearing on international trade? Our farm subsidies are not insignificant (about $30 billion annually, apart from water subsidies); our industrial policy consists of encouraging consumption, no matter how wasteful of money or resources. If the Japanese were squeaky clean, would Americans prosper thereby? Certainly not. The trade imbalance would decrease marginally, if at all. American jobs would still vanish over the Pacific horizon.

Money

Money is a resource also; it is one of the four ingredients essential to economic and productive success: labor, land, capital and raw materials.

It is said that Americans squander this invaluable resource in the pursuit of ego satisfaction and that they must, therefore, accept the consequences. We disagree. We believe that Americans act rationally in their individual self-interest in response to the message they receive in the marketplace. The real problem is that the message of our markets is routinely corrupted by distorted policies.

If the farmer were to forego subsidies as well as to pay the full price for water, other more appropriate crops would be grown, such as cabbages and oranges. The price of rice and cotton would rise; the price of cabbages and oranges would fall. Taxes and the price of urban water would fall. The word "drought" would vanish from our front pages. And the nation's wetlands, marshes and fisheries would be saved.

Incentives

When we are confronted with environmental abuse we commonly conceive of solutions as limited to one of three things: develop new technology to solve the problem (i.e. invent the electric car; use hydrogen as fuel), adopt a command strategy (pass a law requiring that we behave more acceptably), or embark on a program to educate the community to behave more responsibly.

Alone, none of these strategies is effective in resolving such problems. Unless we consider the incentives that really do matter to us, the results are likely to fall far short of our goals. Only an economic (or other believable) strategy will work.

When the correct economic incentives are in place, neither command strategies, education nor directed technological innovation will be necessary. The market will insure that the correct technology will be developed.

An Important Choice

As the Clinton/Gore Administration ponders its choices, it will contemplate its campaign promise to improve the nation's infrastructure; the new directive to spend $156 billion during the next few years will be translated into construction projects.

Will these funds be spent on transit projects for the nation's cities? Or will they produce more urban freeways?

The tempting choice—but the wrong choice—would be to build more highways. The nation's state highway departments are filled with experienced highway personnel. The building trade unions are avid for juicy highway plums. Projects are on the shelf, ready for bidding and the first bull-dozers.

The nation has a surplus of highways. Additional highway capacity would only encourage more automobile and truck trips and a higher-cost economy. Highway engineers arguing for more funds have made the most of the results of deferred maintenance—rusting bridges, broken and potholed pavements. However, when scarce funds are made available the maintenance program is given a low priority. The funds are spent too frequently on constructing new highway capacity.

Reason requires that these funds be used to rebuild and rehabilitate the rail transit systems of the nation, building modern, high-speed intraurban rail systems. If highways must be built, they should be justified honestly as returning at least as much in benefits as they cost in scarce public funds.

Efforts by protagonists to describe new highway projects as attractive investment opportunities are embarrassingly sophomoric. Realistic methodology exists; it is long past time that the highway fraternity adopted it as their public responsibility.

Additional copies of this book may be obtained
from your local bookstore
or by sending $13.95 for a paperback copy, postpaid,
or $18.95 for a hardback library cover copy, postpaid,
to:

**New Paradigm Books
P.O. Box 60008
Pasadena, CA 91116**

CA residents kindly add 8% tax
FAX orders to (818) 792-2121
VISA/MC orders to (800) 326-2671